What Did They Say About Gays?

What Did They Say About Gays?

ALLAN GOULD

ECW PRESS

CANADIAN CATALOGUING IN PUBLICATION DATA

Gould, Allan
What did they say about gays?

ISBN 1-55022-235-X

1. Gays – Quotations. 2. Homosexuality – Quotations, maxims, etc. 3. Quotations, English.
I. Gould, Allan, 1944– .

PN6084.G35W53 1995 082'.08'664 C95-930408-8

Design and imaging by ECW Type & Art, Oakville, Ontario.
Printed by Métropole Litho, Sherbrooke, Québec.

Distributed by General Distribution Services,
30 Lesmill Road, Don Mills, Ontario M3B 2T6.
(416) 445-3333, (800) 387-0172 (Canada), FAX (416) 445-5967.

Distributed to the trade in the United States exclusively
by InBook, 140 Commerce Street, P.O. Box 120261,
East Haven, Connecticut, U.S.A. 06512.
Customer service: (800) 243-0138, FAX (800) 334-3892.

Distributed in Great Britain by Turnaround,
27 Horsell Road, London N5 1XL. (44) 71 6097836.

Published by ECW PRESS,
2120 Queen Street East, Suite 200,
Toronto, Ontario M4E 1E2.

To my beloved wife, Merle, who is as sympathetic to the gay struggle as I am. And to my son, Judah, and daughter, Elisheva, both of whom have a healthy, respectful concern about gay rights, and a profound sense of justice and compassion toward others. What else can parents hope for?

WHAT DID THEY SAY ABOUT GAYS?

A Very Personal Introduction

Without any apology or apologetics or embarrassment, I feel that it's important to begin this essay with a disclaimer: No, I'm not gay. Nor, in an echo of the classic antisemitic line, can I declare hypocritically, "Some of my best friends are gay!" (Although my wife and I have warm acquaintances we treasure, whose sexual orientation — when we eventually discovered it — was no more important to us than their hair colour.)

I come to this book because of my Jewishness, and, not unrelatedly, because of my lifelong involvement in civil rights for blacks. Those three groups, of course, have very much in common: biblical threats and rejection, historical mockery and hatred, long struggles for civil and legal rights, revulsion by society, stonings, lynchings, even murder. The biblical renouncement may not seem as clear for blacks as it is for homosexuals (Leviticus, Romans) and Jews (alas, much of the Christian Testament), but it is still there. When I taught black school children in the 1964 "Freedom Summer" in Mississippi, I was told by dozens of raging white racists, "The nigger is hated in the Bible itself! Doesn't it say that Ham [the son of Noah who looked upon his father's drunken nakedness and laughed, after the ark came to a rest on Mount Ararat] was cursed by God, and that his decendants would be slaves? *There's* the black people, right there!" *I'd* sooner call that a living example of the devil quoting scripture.

As a white Jew growing up in Detroit in the 1940s and 1950s, I was well aware of the widespread mistreatment, segregation, even hatred of blacks, and it enraged me. I can hardly admit the same response to the homosexual community, because to a growing lad struggling with his own raging hormones (as it happened, heterosexual ones), gay people were totally invisible to me. I'm almost embarrassed to write this: my most beloved high-school instructor, who influenced me most in terms of choosing teaching literature and writing books as a career, was obviously gay — but only in retrospect, so that, as a man in my thirties, I was actually surprised to hear of his homosexuality from my closest high-school chum. No, when it comes to any interest in — much less awareness of — the gay community and its history, pains, and struggles, I am a very late bloomer, indeed.

One more confession: I can think of only a single reference to homosexuality from my youth, and it's not a particularly attractive one, at least in terms of modelling my behaviour. My late father, then probably in his late fifties, told his then-teenaged younger son of an incident that occurred in his twenties. He had once entered a washroom, and while relieving himself at the urinal, a man looked at him, pointed at his organ, and declared, "Boy, I'd like to suck that!" My father looked at me proudly as he exclaimed, "I told that idiot, 'How'd you like me to break your goddamn neck?' " Interestingly, I remember thinking, "What an ugly, violent response. I would just tell the guy to get lost."

The point I'm making, with this unpleasant memory of my decent but Old School father (born in 1904 in Russia, embittered by the antisemitism he had encountered in his youth, but always sensitive and caring towards the black community, which he felt got far worse deals than he ever did), is that I was clearly open for tolerance — if not a heartfelt acceptance — of the gay community at a fairly young age.

Back to my own history, where it's relevant: I earned my bachelor's degree at Wayne State University in Detroit, my master's (in theatre and theatre history) at New York University Graduate School of Arts and Science, and my Ph.D. in English at York University in Toronto (after marrying a Canadian-born woman and moving up here in 1968), taught university for several years, wrote for and performed on dozens of radio and TV shows, and finally — I really am a late bloomer — I discovered my forte in 1981, when I began to write magazine articles, and eventually books, full-time.

My nineteenth book, which I began in the late 1980s and saw published in 1991, was *What Did They Think of the Jews?* As I put together this heavy tome (more than six hundred pages, heaven help me, and with a retail cost of $50) for an American publisher, I was struck by a touching fact — some of the most sensitive, philo-Semitic essays, letters, and declarations I uncovered were from men who were homosexual. And, probably not unrelated, many of the most vicious, antisemitic ravings were from people who also spoke vehemently against homosexuality.

The generous response of gays towards Jews was almost universal. Here's E.M. Forster, in an essay in *The New Statesman* in early 1939, as Europe marched towards war: "To me, anti-Semitism is now the most shocking of all things. It is destroying much more than the Jews; it is assailing the human mind at its source, and inviting it to create false categories before exercising judgment. . . ."

Thornton Wilder, writing to a woman who had spewed hatred towards Jews in her request for an autograph: "The first sentence of your letter made me shudder so that I keep it by me all the time to remind me of how slowly the world is learning the lessons by which it must live and pursue happiness and attain peace."

Not that one must be a homosexual to feel for the anguish of the Jews; the strongest, most deeply felt and articulate praise of the Jewish people and religion in my massive anthology was from two well-known heterosexual authors, Mark Twain and Leo Tolstoy. Still, I found it informative that one of the most insightful essays on the eternal question of Jew-hatred came from Havelock Ellis, the British physician, scientist, and social reformer who probably did more to enlighten the world about homosexuality than any other human being in the past century. Here is what Ellis wrote, shortly before his death in the 1930s, in an essay called "The Jewish Question":

> [T]hose who seek to injure the Jews in the end only injure themselves and benefit the world. . . . So I expect to see the Jews still carrying on successfully, much as they have any time during the past three thousand years. . . .
>
> Looking broadly at the matter, even with but a small knowledge of human nature, it is easy to account for anti-Semitism. The four thinkers to whom, above all others, we owe the development of the modern spirit have been Jews: Marx, Bergson, Freud, and Einstein.

I do not mean to imply that all Jews and all homosexuals are "brothers"; indeed, one of the most bitter essays I encountered in my earlier anthology on the Jews was by Gore Vidal, the famous novelist and proud gay man, who wrote angrily in *The Nation* ("Pink Triangle and Yellow Star") in 1989:

> Like it or not, Jews and homosexualists are in the same fragile boat, and one would have to be pretty obtuse not to see the common danger. But obtuseness is the name of the game among New York's new class. Elsewhere, I have described the shrill fag-baiting of Joseph Epstein, Norman Podhoretz. . . . *Harper's* magazine and *Commentary* usually publish these pieces. . . . Since [right-wing Jews] are going to be in the same gas chambers as the blacks and the faggots, I would suggest a cease-fire and a common front against the common enemy, whose kindly voice is that of Ronald Reagan and whose less than kindly mind is elsewhere in the boardrooms of the Republic.

No, dear reader, I am hardly about to declare that Jews and gays are automatically friends (like the cowboy and the rancher in *Oklahoma*). Misery often does not only *not* like company, but usually resents others who complain. (Some of the greatest hatreds I have encountered in my life have been Puerto Ricans for blacks in New York, each of them struggling against racism and fighting for a rung on the greased ladder.)

Back to my opening thought. I wrote *What Did They Think of the Jews?* as a Jew who had always been intrigued, even obsessed, with the universal sickness of antisemitism and the rare examples of philo-Semitism. I approached *this* work from the same intellectual if not deeply personal perspective. Why has the world always had such difficulties in accepting differences in sexual orientation? What are the religious origins for this (Babylonian, Jewish, Buddhist, Zoroastrian, Christian, Islamic)? Who were the haters of gays, and why? Who were the (less common, but still, surprisingly, often there) defenders, and why? After all, if you don't know who your enemies are, and where they are coming from, and you don't know who your friends are, can you ever truly be safe and secure in your sexuality and life?

Many documents in these pages will be familiar. Is there any literate person who does not know the (probably misrepresented) story of Sodom and Gomorrah from the Hebrew Testament? Others are surprisingly less well known, at least to this anthologizer: Sigmund Freud's letter to an American mother in 1935, written in English, is so seminal, I am surprised that it is not reprinted on the cover of every gay magazine and newspaper in the world: "Homosexuality is assuredly no advantage, but it is nothing to be ashamed of, no vice, no degradation, it cannot be classified as an illness. . . . It is a great injustice to persecute homosexuality as a crime, and cruelty, too."

There are some real shockers in this book, at least to this sympathetic heterosexual anthologizer. I was charmed by Montaigne's sixteenth-century essay; stunned by the three hundred pages — unpublished in his lifetime, naturally — scrawled by the brilliant utilitarian philosopher Jeremy Bentham, who defended homosexuality with both passion and logic; moved by Edmund Burke's dangerous rejection of the stoning of homosexuals in the House of Commons (this, from the father of modern conservatism!); and I had to laugh at those identical twins who have influenced the tastes and mores of hundreds of millions — "Dear Abby" and "Ann Landers" — who ended up on opposite sides of the issue, the former a passionate defender of gays, the latter sticking to her "homosexuality is a sickness" argument.

In anthologizing and editing a book like this, one must have guidelines, and I chose to follow two. First, few, if any, writings from fiction; and second, and most important, no comments from homosexuals.

Let me defend each of these choices. The first is easy: you *cannot* always judge people's feelings about a religion, race, or sex by what they write. Scholars call this "the intentional fallacy," which merely means that it is fallacious to assume an author's true intentions. Writers have the right to create a Jewish black gay villain without necessarily being antisemitic, racist, or homophobic. Indeed, while Shakespeare probably never met a Jew in his life (Jews having been expelled from England in 1290), he managed to create a far more sympathetic portrait of a Jew — and a far harsher depiction of Christians — than had most other artists of his age in any medium. (Be sure to read Norman Mailer's heartfelt, if naïve, apologia for his frequently negative gay characters in his early novels, which was first written for the gay magazine *One* in the mid-1950s, reprinted in this book.)

My second decision is more debatable, so please allow me to explain. If you wish to read what Plato or Leonardo or Gide or Vidal wrote about same-sex love, countless books present their writings. I wanted to put as many key, important, insightful, and relevant comments, laws, insults, or defences about or of homosexuality made by heterosexuals as I could between two covers, so that people could finally, *finally* see who their enemies were (are), and who their friends were (are), and how times have (or haven't) changed. That, to me, is the value of this book. There may be the rare exception, such as the tortured views of the gifted Soviet filmmaker Sergei Eisenstein, who struggled over whether he may have been a homosexual, and his dreadful fears seemed sadly relevant to this book. And I may well have included a gay or two, without knowing it. This, in itself, is a comment about how necessary gays have found it to hide their sexual identity.

So here you have it: what more than one hundred men and women have said or written or felt about homosexuals and homosexuality in the past three thousand years. Sexuality is a scary thing. It cuts to the core of who we are and how we see the world. By reading what straights have written about homosexuality over three-plus millennia, we can learn quite a bit about how far we have come, and how far we still have to go.

Allan Gould
Toronto, Canada
Winter, 1994–95

MINNESOTA MULTIPHASIC PERSONALITY INVENTORY

A test that attempts to assess personalities by asking 550 true–false questions.

[Within this widely used test, there is a scale designed to pick out male homosexuals by the way in which they reply. It is called the Mf scale.

The first list, below, supposedly tends to evoke a "true" reply from homosexuals, and the second a "false" reply.]

TRUE

I think I would like the work of a librarian.
I used to like drop-the-handkerchief.
I have often wished I were a girl.
I like poetry.
I would like to be a florist.
I would like to be a nurse.
I like collecting flowers or growing house plants.
I like to cook.
I used to keep a diary.
If I were a reporter I would very much like to report news of the theater.
I would like to be a journalist.
If I were an artist I would like to draw flowers.
I like "Alice in Wonderland" by Lewis Carroll.

FALSE

I like mechanics magazines.
My feelings are not easily hurt.
I do not have a great fear of snakes.
I daydream very little.
I have never had any breaking out on my skin that has worried me.
I like science.
I believe there is a Devil and a Hell in afterlife.
I am entirely self-confident.
There never was a time in my life when I liked to play with dolls.

¶ Quoted in *Homosexuality: A Philosophical Inquiry* by Michael Ruse (London: Basil Blackwell, 1988), p. 218.

From the Babylonians to the Foundations of Christianity

THE SUMMA ALU

An ancient Babylonian manual for divining the future.

If a man has intercourse with the hindquarters of his equal [male], that man will be foremost among his brothers and colleagues.

If a man yearns to express his manhood while in prison and thus, like a male cult-prostitute, mating with men becomes his desire, he will experience evil.

If a man has intercourse with a [male] cult prostitute, care [trouble] will leave him.

If a man has intercourse with a [male] courtier, for one whole year the worry which plagued him will vanish.

If a man has intercourse with a [male] slave, care will seize him.

None of the acts elicits moral condemnation, but some are auspicious whereas others are not. Homosexuality itself carries no implications; neither here nor anywhere else does the concept of a homosexual person even appear. What matters are the roles and statuses of the parties. To penetrate someone of high social status (an equal, a cult prostitute, a courtier) anally is favorable; to be involved with one's slave, unfavorable. The Babylonians may have felt that a sexual connection would erode a master's authority over his slaves. . . .

¶ From *The Construction of Homosexuality* by David F. Greenberg (Chicago: University of Chicago Press, 1988), pp. 126–27.

MIDDLE ASSYRIAN LAW

Circa 2500 BC.

If a seignior started a rumor against his neighbor in private, saying "People have lain repeatedly with him," or he said to him in a brawl in the presence of [other] people, "People have lain repeatedly with you; I will prosecute you," since he is not able to prosecute [him] [and] did not prosecute [him], they shall flog that seignior fifty [times] with staves [and] he shall do the work of the king for one full month; they shall castrate him and he shall also pay one talent of lead.

¶ Quoted in *The Construction of Homosexuality* by David F. Greenberg (Chicago: University of Chicago Press 1988), p. 125.

OLD [HEBREW] TESTAMENT

The original mention of the term "sodomy."

And there came two angels to Sodom at even: and Lot sat in the gate of Sodom: and Lot seeing them rose up to meet them; and he bowed himself with his face toward the ground;

And he said, Behold now, my lords, turn in, I pray you, into your servant's house, and tarry all night, and wash your feet, and ye shall rise up early, and go on your ways. And they said, Nay; but we will abide in the street all night.

And he pressed upon them greatly; and they turned in unto him, and entered into his house; and he made them a feast, and did bake unleavened bread, and they did eat.

But before they lay down, the men of the city, even the men of Sodom, compassed the house round, both old and young, all the people from every quarter:

And they called unto Lot, and said unto him, Where are the men which came in to thee this night? Bring them out unto us, that we may know* them.

And Lot went out at the door unto them, and shut the door after them,

And said, I pray you, brethren, do not so wickedly.

Behold now, I have two daughters which have not known man; let me, I pray you, bring them out unto you, and do ye to them as is good in your eyes: only unto these men do nothing; for therefore came they under the shadow of my roof.

And they said, Stand back. And they said again, This one fellow came in to sojourn, and he will needs be a judge: now will we deal worse with thee, than with them. And they pressed sore upon the man, even Lot, and came near to break the door.

But the men put forth their hand, and pulled Lot into the house to them, and shut to the door.

---

* According to painstaking research by several scholars in recent years, it has been widely noted that the Hebrew word for "know" — usually taken to assume that the people of Sodom wanted to have sexual knowledge with the angel-visitors of Lot — actually occurs 943 times in the Old Testament, yet is used in that sexual sense only 15 times. In nearly every occasion, it means simply "become acquainted with."

And they smote the men that were at the door of the house with blindness, both small and great: so that they were wearied themselves to find the door.

And the men said unto Lot, Hast thou here any besides? Son-in-law, and thy sons, and thy daughters, and whatsoever thou hast in the city, bring them out of this place;

For we will destroy this place, because the cry of them is waxen great before the face of the Lord; and the Lord hath sent us to destroy it.

¶ From Genesis 19:1–13.

And Er, Judah's first born, was wicked in the sight of the Lord: and the Lord slew him.

And Judah said unto Onan, Go in unto thy brother's wife, and marry her, and raise up the seed to thy brother.

And Onan knew that the seed should not be his; and it came to pass, when he went in unto his brother's wife, that he spilled it on the ground, lest that he should give seed to his brother.

And the thing which he did displeased the Lord; whereupon He slew him also.

¶ From Genesis 38:7–10.

Thou shalt not lie with mankind, as with womankind: it is an abomination.

¶ From Leviticus 18:22.

If a man also lie with mankind, as he lieth with a woman, both of them have committed an abomination; they shall surely be put to death; and their blood shall be upon them.

¶ From Leviticus 21:13.

There shall be no whore of the daughters of Israel, nor a sodomite of the sons of Israel.

Thou shalt not bring the hire of a whore, or the price of a dog, into the house of the Lord thy God for any vow: for even both these are abomination unto the Lord thy God.

¶ From Deuteronomy 23:17–18.

And Judah did evil in the sight of the Lord, and they provoked him to jealousy with their sins which they had committed, above all that their fathers had done.

For they also built them high places, and images, and groves, on every high hill, and under every green tree.

And there were also sodomites in the land: and they did according to all the abominations of the nations which the Lord cast out before the children of Israel.

¶ From 1 Kings 14:22–24.

And Asa did that which was right in the eyes of the Lord, as did David his father.

And he took away the sodomites out of the land, and removed all the idols that his fathers had made.

¶ From 1 Kings 15:11–12.

BABYLONIAN TALMUD

Jewish religious commentary upon the Hebrew Testament, 200–500 AD.

He who does not engage in propagation of the race is as though he has shed blood.

¶ From *Tractate Yevamot* 63b.

The generation of Noah, according to midrashic teaching, was condemned to eradication by the Flood because they had sunk so low morally, they wrote out formal marriage contracts for sodomy and buggery.

¶ From *Leviticus Rabba* 18:13.

On the scriptural story of Potiphar's purchase of Joseph as a slave (Genesis 39:1), the Talmud comments that he acquired him for homosexual purposes, but that a miracle occurred and God sent the angel Gabriel to castrate Potiphar.

¶ From *Sota* 13b.

Rabbi Judah [the codifier of the Mishna] forbade two bachelors from sleeping under the same blanket, for fear that this would lead to homosexual temptation.

¶ From *Kiddushin* 4:14.

The Sages permitted the above, however, because homosexuality was "so rare among Jews that such preventative legislation was considered unnecessary."

¶ From *Kiddushin* 82a.

BUDDHISM

Spiritual tradition of northern India, founded in the sixth century BC *by Siddhartha Gautama, "the Buddha," or "Awakened One."*

The lay moral code (*Pancasila*) leaves it up to the individual to interpret what such misconduct might be, but the supplementary texts spell out such offenses as adultery, rape, and taking advantage of those over whom one exercises authority. What is *not* included even in the supplementary canonical texts is any condemnation of pre-marital sex or of homosexuality as such. In short, the unmarried Buddhist layperson is free to engage in consensual homosexual acts. This had led to a great deal of tolerance of homosexuality in modern Buddhist countries.

The monastic code of discipline or *vinaya*, however, is aimed at curtailing all passions, including sexual ones. "Is not the Law taught by me for the allaying of the fever of pleasures of the senses?" explains the Buddha in a canonical *vinaya* text. Thus all acts involving the intentional emission of his semen are prohibited for the monk; the insertion of the penis into a female or male is grounds for automatic expulsion from the *Sangha*, while even masturbation is a (lesser) offense. On the other hand, the *vinaya* is silent on matters which presumably were not thought to arouse the sense-pleasures; thus there is no law against a monk receiving a penis into his own body. While a monk is prohibited by lesser rules from even touching the body of a female (even a female animal), no such rule pertains to other males, and the physical expression of affection is very common among the Buddhist monks.

. . . Interestingly, while a novice [monk] commits a grave offense if he engages in coitus with a female, requiring him to leave the *Sangha*, should he instead have sex with a male he is only guilty of a lesser offense requiring that he reaffirm his *samanera* vows and perform such penance as is directed by his teacher. This may be the only instance of a world religion treating homosexual acts more favorably than heterosexual ones.

¶ From *Encyclopedia of Homosexuality*, ed. Wayne R. Dynes (New York: Garland, 1990), p. 169.

ZOROASTRIANISM

The most important indigenous religion of ancient Iran, it reached its peak between 500 BC and 300 BC.

In ancient Iran, homosexual behavior was forbidden by religious law. Although the Prophet of Zoroastrianism, Zarathustra Spitama, did not specifically list "do's" and "don'ts" in his hymns, the . . . Gathas, which was composed by Magian priests centuries later, vehemently attack homosexuality. In the Vendidad, "Laws Against Evil" described those who committed sodomy as demons, with severe punishments set forth against them:

> O Maker of the material world, Thou Holy One! Who is the man that is a demon? Who is he that is the worshipper of the devil? . . .
>
> Ahura Mazda replied: "The man that lies with mankind as man lies with womankind. . . ."
>
> O Maker of the material world, Thou Holy One! If a man willfully commits sodomy what is the penalty for it? What is the atonement for it? What is the cleansing from it? . . .
>
> Ahura Mazda replied: "For that deed there is nothing that can pay, nothing that can atone, nothing that can cleanse from it; it is a trespass for which there is no atonement for ever and ever."

A full millennium after the composition of the Vendidad, the attitude of medieval literature continued to reflect hostility. In the book Menog I Khrad

("Spirit of Wisdom"), a compilation of the later Sasanian period (circa fifth century AD), the following was proclaimed:

> The sage asked the spirit of wisdom thus: "Which sin is the more heinous?"
>
> The spirit of wisdom answered thus: "Of the sin which people commit, unnatural [homosexual] intercourse is the most heinous. The second is he who has suffered or performed intercourse with men. The third, who slays a righteous man. . . .

¶ From *Menog I Khrad* 36:2.

The official view on homosexuality, as promulgated by Zoroastrian priesthood in ancient times, was that homosexuality was directly attributable to the Evil Spirit, and all means were to be used to destroy evil. In the commentary to the Vendidad, it is stated that sodomites, highway robbers, and those guilty of burning corpses could be put to death without a trial (8:73–74).

Since the medieval period, however, these views have been limited only to the pages of ancient texts, and, even earlier, the extent of the execution of homosexuals is questionable. By the ninth century AD, a homosexual could repent his "sin" and ensure his entry into paradise (Dadestan I Denig 75:5). During this period, homosexuals were shunned by society, since the ancient belief that their actions pollute the Good creation of Ahura Mazda still prevailed.

Today, homosexuality continues to be regarded by many Zoroastrians as contrary to religious law. Active ostracism of homosexuals, however, does not occur. There are those among Zoroastrian intellectuals who believe that someday there may be a scientific explanation for homosexual behavior, so they adhere to the idea that the pristine teachings of their Prophet as evident in the Gathas were designed to be timeless. Thus, they purposely leave out such discreet matters to allow the believers to advance with changing times through new acquired knowledge, without compromising the basic principles of the religion.

¶ From "Purity and Pollution in Zoroastrianism: Triumph over Evil" by Jamsheed Choksey, in *Sacred Books of the East*, ed. F. Max Müeller, vol. 2.

PHILO JUDAEUS (20 BC–50 AD)

Early Jewish philosopher.

[The men of Sodom had ignored the law of nature] and applied themselves to deep drinking of strong liquor and dainty feeding and forbidden forms of intercourse. Not only in their mad lust for women did they violate the marriage of their neighbors, but also men mounted males without respect for the sex nature which the active partner shares with the passive; and so when they tried to beget children they were discovered to be incapable of any but a sterile seed. Yet the discovery availed them not, so much stronger was the force of lust which mastered them. Then, as little by little they accustomed those who were by nature men to submit to play the part of women, they saddled them with the formidable curse of a female disease. For not only did they emasculate their bodies by luxury and voluptuousness, but they worked a further degeneration in their soul and, so far as in them lay, were corrupting the whole of mankind.

¶ From *On Abraham*, trans. F.H. Colson, Loeb Classical Library (London: William Heinemann, 1959–62), vol. 4, chap. 26, pp. 134–36.

PLINY THE ELDER (23–79 AD)

Caius Plinius Secundus, Latin author.

Transformation of females into males is not an idle story. We find in the Annals that in the consulship of Publius Licinius Crassus and Gaius Cassius Longinus [171 BC] a girl at Casinum was changed into a boy, under the observation of the parents, and at the order of the augurs was conveyed away to a desert island. Licinius Mucianus has recorded that he personally saw at Argos a man named Arescon who had been given the name of Arescusa and had actually married a husband, and then had grown a beard and developed masculine attributes and had taken a wife; and that he had also seen a boy with the same record at Smyrna. I myself saw in Africa a person who had turned into a male on the day of marriage to a husband; this was Lucius Constitus, a citizen of Thysdritium.

¶ From *Natural History*, trans. H. Rackham, Loeb Classical Library (Cambridge: Harvard University Press, 1967–80), vol. 2, bk. 7, sec. 4.

TERTULLIAN

Early church leader, circa early third century AD.

[Those who engage in] all the other frenzies of passions [other than adultery and fornication] . . . beyond the laws of nature [should be banished] not only from the threshold, but from all shelter of the Church, because they are not sins, but monstrosities.

¶ Quoted in *The Construction of Homosexuality* by David F. Greenberg (Chicago: University of Chicago Press, 1988), p. 218.

PLUTARCH (46–120 AD)

Greek biographer and essayist.

. . . The noble lover of beauty engages in love wherever he sees excellence and splendid natural endowment without regard for any difference in physiological detail.

[He will be] fairly and equably disposed toward both sexes, instead of supposing that males and females are as different in the matter of love as they are in their clothes.

¶ From *Erotikos*, or *Dialogue on Love.*

NEW [CHRISTIAN] TESTAMENT

Know ye not that the unrighteous shall not inherit the Kingdom of God? Be not deceived: neither fornicators, nor idolators, nor adulterers, nor effeminate, nor abusers of themselves with mankind,

Nor thieves, nor covetous, nor drunkards, nor revilers, nor extortioners, shall inherit the Kingdom of God.

¶ From 1 Corinthians 6:9–10.

Knowing this, that the law is not made for a righteous man, but for the lawless and disobedient, for the ungodly and for sinners, for the unholy and profane, for murderers of fathers and murderers of mothers, for manslayers,

For whoremongers, for them that defile themselves with mankind, for menstealers, for liars, for perjured persons, and if there be any other thing that is contrary to sound doctrine.

¶ From 1 Timothy 1:9–10.

For this cause God gave them up into vile affections: for even their women did change the natural use into that which is against nature:

And likewise also the men, leaving the natural use of the woman, burned in their lust one toward another; men with men working that which is unseemly, and receiving in themselves that recompense of their error which was meet.

And even as they did not like to retain God in their knowledge, God gave them over to a reprobate mind, to do those things that are not convenient;

Being filled with all unrighteousness, fornication, wickedness, covetousness, maliciousness; fully of envy, murder, debate, deceit, malignity; whisperers,

Backbiters, haters of God, despiteful, proud, boasters, inventors of evil things, disobedient to parents,

Without understanding, covenant-breakers, without natural affection, implacable, unmerciful:

Who, knowing the judgment of God, that which they commit such things are worthy of death, not only do the same, but have pleasure in them that do them.

¶ From Romans 1:26–32.

These two quotations have traditionally been seen as referring to homosexuals.

But the fearful, and unbelieving, and the abominable, and murderers, and whoremongers, and sorcerers, and idolaters, and all liars, shall have their part in the lake which burneth with fire and brimstone, which is the second death.

¶ From Revelation 21:8.

For without are dogs, and sorcerers, and whoremongers, and murderers, and idolaters, and whosoever loveth and maketh a lie.

¶ From Revelation 22:15.

SAINT BASIL OF NYSSA

Fourth-century theologian, founder of Christian monasticism.

He who is guilty of unseemliness with males will be under discipline for the same time as adulterers.

¶ From a letter to another bishop, 375 AD.

Fly from intimate association with comrades your own age and run away from them as from fire. The enemy has indeed set many aflame through such means and consigned them down into that loathsome pit of the five cities (Genesis 1:19; Deuteronomy 29:23) on the pretext of spiritual love. . . .

At meals take a seat far away from your young brother; in lying down to rest, let not your garments be neighbor to his; rather, have an elderly brother lying between you. When a young brother converses with you or is opposite you in choir, make your response with your head bowed lest per chance by gazing fixedly into his face, the seed of desire be implanted in you by the wicked sower and you reap sheaves of corruption and ruin. At home or in a place where there is no witness of your actions, be not found in his company under the pretext of meditation on the Divine Word or for any other excuse, even the most urgent need.

¶ From "De renuntiatione saeculi" ("On the Renunciation of the World"), *The Fathers of the Church*, vol. 9, pp. 23–24.

JOHN CHRYSOSTOM (345–407 AD)

Father of early Greek church, elected archbishop of Constantinople in 398.

Those very people who have been nourished by godly doctrine, who instruct others in what they ought and ought not to do, who have heard the Scriptures brought down from heaven, these do not consort with prostitutes as fearlessly as they do with young men. . . . None is ashamed. . . . Indeed . . . [T]here is some danger that womankind will become unnecessary in the future, with young men instead fulfilling all the needs women used to.

¶ From *Against the Opponents of the Monastic Life*, 3.8.

SAINT AUGUSTINE (354–430 AD)

Early church father and philosopher.

. . . [T]hose shameful acts against nature, such as were committed in Sodom, ought everywhere and always to be detested and punished. If all nations were to do such things, they would be held guilty of the same crime by the law of God, which has not so made men that they should use one another in this way.

¶ From *The Confessions*, bk. 3, chap. 8.

THEODOSIUS, VALENTINIAN II, ARCADIUS

Three Roman emperors who shared the throne in 390 AD.

All persons who have the shameful custom of condemning a man's body, acting the part of a woman's, to the sufferance of an alien sex (for they appear not to be different from women) shall expiate a crime of this kind by avenging flames in the sight of the people [the death penalty for anal intercourse].

¶ From *The Theodosian Code*, trans. Clyde Pharr (Princeton, N.J.: Princeton University Press, 1952), pp. 137–38.

From the Middle Ages
to the Renaissance

EMPEROR JUSTINIAN (483–565 AD)

Byzantine emperor.

[Citizens must abstain from] that abominable and impious conduct deservedly hated by God. We speak of the defilement of males which some men sacrilegiously and impiously dare to attempt, perpetrating vile acts upon other men. For instructed by the Holy Scriptures, we know that God brought a just judgment upon those who lived in Sodom, on account of this very madness of intercourse, so that to this very day the land burns with inextinguishable fire. . . . If, with eyes as if were blinded, we overlook such impious and forbidden contact, we may provoke the good God to anger and bring ruin upon all — a fate which would be but deserved.

¶ From "Novel, CXLI," quoted in *Homosexuality and the Western Christian Tradition* by Derrick Sherwin Bailey (London: Longmans, Green, 1955), pp. 74–75.

KING EGICA (687–701 AD)

Visigoth leader.

[From the Council of Toledo, a major early church gathering, Spain, 693 AD]:

Among other matters, see that you determine to extirpate that obscene crime committed by those who lie with males, whose fearful conduct defiles the charm of honest living and provokes from heaven the wrath of the supreme Judge.

If any one of these males who commit this vile practice against nature with other males is a bishop, a priest, or a deacon, he shall be degraded from the dignity of his order, and shall remain in perpetual exile, struck down by damnation.* Moreover, if any have been implicated in the evils of another's filthy doings, let them be punished nonetheless, without respect of order, rank, or person, by the sentence of the law which was enacted concerning

* Penalties included one hundred lashes, a shaven head, and banishment from Spain. The King later added castration to the church penalties.

such offences, and let them be excluded from all communion with Christians, and furthermore let them be punished with one hundred stripes of the lash, shorn of their hair, as a mark of disgrace, and banished in perpetual exile. . . .

¶ From *Concilium Toletanum* (Council of Toledo, 693 AD).

CUMMEAN PENITENTIAL

French (Frankish) religious manual for priests of the seventh century.

KISSING *Offenders under 20 years of age:*
"Simple kissing." Six special fasts.
"Licentious kissing." Without emission, eight special fasts.
Kissing "with emission or embrace." Ten special fasts.
Offenders over twenty years of age:
There was no distinction made here. The penance was to live in continence, eat separately (on bread and water), and to be excluded from the church; the length of it was presumably at the discretion of the confessor.
MUTUAL MASTURBATION *By men over twenty:*
Twenty or forty days' penance.
One hundred days for a second offense.
If habitual, "the persons concerned are to be separated and to do penance for a full year."
INTERFEMORAL CONNECTION *(insertion of the penis between the thighs of the passive partner):*
A penance of two years.
Or 100 days for the first offense and one year for the second. . . .
FELLATIO *(oral intercourse):*
A penance of four years.
For habitual offenders, seven years.
SODOMY *(anal intercourse):*
Seven years' penance.

¶ From *Sex in History* by Reay Tannahill (New York: Stein and Day, 1980), pp. 158–59.

POPE GREGORY III (d. 741 AD)

Saint.

[Sodomy is] a vice so abominable in the sight of God, that the cities in which its practitioners dwelt were appointed for destruction by fire and brimstone.

¶ From *Judicia Greg Pap* III, 21, quoted in *Homosexuality and the Western Christian Tradition*, by Derrick Sherwin Bailey (London: Longmans, Green, 1955), p. 106.

THE KORAN

The Holy Writ of Islam.

O my people, I did convey to you the message of my Lord and gave you good advice, but you love not being advised. Lot, whom We sent, rebuked his people: Do you realise you practise an abomination of which no people in the world before you has been guilty? You approach men lustfully in place of women. You are a people who exceed all bounds.

¶ From *The Quran*, trans. Muhammad Zafrulla Khan (New York: Olive Branch, 1991), 7:80–81.

To Lot also we gave wisdom and knowledge and We delivered him from the city which practised abominations. They were indeed a wicked and rebellious people.

¶ From *The Quran*, trans. Muhammad Zafrulla Khan (New York: Olive Branch, 1991), 21:74.

Out of all creation have you selected only males for yourselves, and do you leave aside your wives whom your Lord created for you? You are a people who transgress the limits set by nature. They retorted: If thou desist not, Lot, thou wilt surely be banished. He observed: Certainly I detest your practice; and he prayed: Lord, deliver me and my family from their vile conduct. So We delivered him and his family, all of them, except an old woman who stayed behind. Then We destroyed the rest. We sent upon them a rain of stones, and evil is the rain that descends upon those who are warned and disregard the warning. In that surely is a Sign; but most of these would not believe. Surely, it is thy Lord Who is the Mighty, the Ever Merciful.

¶ From *The Quran,* trans. Muhammad Zafrulla Khan (New York: Olive Branch, 1991), 26:171–76.

We also sent Lot who admonished his people: Do you commit evil deliberately? Do you approach men lustfully rather than women? You are indeed a perverse people. The only answer of his people was: Drive out Lot and his family from the city. They are people who take pride in their purity.

¶ From *The Quran,* trans. Muhammad Zafrulla Khan (New York: Olive Branch, 1991), 27:55–56.

We sent Lot to his people and he admonished them: You commit an abomination which none among mankind has ever committed before you. Do you indeed approach men lustfully, and commit highway robberies and behave indecently in your meetings? The only response of his people was: Then bring upon us the chastisement of Allah, if thou speakest the truth. Lot prayed: Lord, help me against this wicked people.

¶ From *The Quran,* trans. Muhammad Zafrulla Khan (New York: Olive Branch, 1991), 29:29–32.

THE HADITH

A tenth-century compilation about the prophet Muhammad's life and sayings, from the Arabic, "saying or tradition."

Whenever a male mounts another male, the throne of God trembles.

[The angels glance down in disgust and cry] "Lord, why do you not command the earth to punish them and the heaven to rain stones on them?"

God: "I am forbearing; nothing will escape me."

If you see two people who act like the people of Lot, then kill the active and the passive.

¶ From *The Hadith.*

ST. THOMAS AQUINAS (1225–1274)

Italian scholastic theologian and philosopher.

It must be said that the more a thing is necessary the more crucial it is that it be regulated by reason and consequently the greater the evil if that order of reason is violated. However as we have already stated sexual acts are very necessary for the common good which is the survival of the race. Therefore concerning them the greatest attention must be paid to the ordering of reason. Consequently if anything is done in connection with them against the order of reason it is a sin. And so without any doubt lust is sin.

To the first objection it must be said that according to Aristotle in the same book *semen is a surplus* which is necessary, he says it is a surplus insofar as it is a residue of the action of the nutrient power yet it is necessary regarding the generative power. The other waste-products of the body are not necessary and therefore it does not matter how they are disposed of provided the decencies of social life are observed. But it is different with the emission of semen which must be done in the way befitting the end for which it is needed. . . .

It should be mentioned . . . that the sin of lechery consists in this — that a person engages in venereal pleasure not in accordance with the right reason. This can happen in two ways: one is respect to the substance of the act in which the pleasure is sought. The other in which the act is proper but other conditions are not met. . . .

. . . [U]ncleanness stands for lust against nature, while lewdness pertains to corruption of the young which is a form of seduction. Or we can also say that lewdness pertains to those various acts surrounding the sex-act such as kissing, caressing and the like.

[Homosexuality] is contrary to the natural order of the venereal act as befits human species and this is why it is called the unnatural vice. It can happen in various ways. First by having orgasm outside of intercourse for the sake of venereal pleasure which pertains to the sin of uncleanness which some call effeminacy [this probably refers to masturbation]. Secondly by copulating with another species which is called bestiality. Thirdly by copulating with the wrong sex, male with male or female with female as St. Paul states (Romans 1:27) and this is the vice of sodomy. Fourthly, by not observing the natural manner of copulation either as to not using the proper organ or as to other monstrous and bestial manners of copulation. . . .

The lustful man intends not human generation but venereal pleasure. It is possible without those acts from which human generation follow: and it is this which is sought in unnatural acts. . . .

And so a sin against nature in which the natural order itself is violated is a sin against God who is the creator of that order. Augustine writes, "Offenses against nature should be abhorred and punished always and in every case. Such as those committed by the people of Sodom which if every nation committed them they would be held just as guilty by the same divine law which never intended that men treat one another in such a fashion. "For the fellowship which should exist between God and man would be destroyed when nature which is God's handiwork is made foul by the perversity of lust."

¶ From *Summa Theologica*, pp. 1265–73.

NICCOLO MACHIAVELLI (1469–1527)

Florentine statesman and political philosopher (THE PRINCE).

Though Niccolo's military writings discuss what kinds of love or fear might hold the soldier fast and fierce in battle, they never seek it in homosexual affection in the ranks. Not that pederasty is unfamiliar. Niccolo has homosexual friends. Several of his wonderful storytelling letters of the winter of 1513–1514 detail some of their comings and goings, telling us how common a theme homosexuality is. In one, Niccolo confirms that his leaning is in the opposite direction. Vettori in Rome had been complaining of his houseguests and their discordant tastes. They had driven his usual pleasures out the door. Niccolo writes back that with such a scene of austerity, perhaps he ought to appear there to clarify things, for "I lay hand on and cater to women." On seeing the cheerless house he would say, "Ambassador, you must be sick; I don't think you're having any fun; here there is no boy, here there are no girls; what kind of a fucking house is this?"

¶ From *Machiavelli in Hell* by Sebastian de Grazia (New York: Random House, 1989).

MARTIN LUTHER (1483–1546)

Religious leader of the Protestant Reformation.

The heinous conduct of the people of Sodom is extraordinary, in as much as they departed from the natural passion and longing of the male for the female, which was implanted by God, and desired what is altogether contrary to nature. Whence comes this perversity? Undoubtedly from Satan, who, after people have once turned away from the fear of God, so powerfully suppresses nature that he beats out the natural desire and stirs up a desire that is contrary to nature.

¶ From "Lectures on Genesis," in *Works*, ed. Jaroslav Pelikan and Helmut Lehmann (Philadelphia and St. Louis: Mullenberg and Concordia, 1955–1967), 3:255.

JOSEPH KARO (1488–1575)

Codifier of Jewish law.

In our times, when lewdness is rampant, one should abstain from being alone with another male.

¶ From *Shulchan Aruch* (*The Set Table*).

KING HENRY VIII (1491–1547)

Henry Tudor, second of the Tudor Kings,
King of England, 1509–1547.

Forasmuch as there is not yet sufficient and Condyne punishment apoynted and limited by the due course of the Lawes of this Realme for the detestable and abominable Vice of Buggery committed with mankind or beast . . . that the same offence be from henceforth adjudged felony and such order and form of process therein to be used agaynst the offenders as in cases of felony at the Common lawe. And that the offenders being hereof convict by verdict confession or outlawry shall suffer such paynes of death and losses and penalties of their goods chattels debts lands tenements and hereditaments as felons being accustomed to do accordynge to the order of the Common Lawes of this Realme. . . .*

¶ From *The Act of 25 Henry* VIII, chap. 6.

GRAND DUCHESS MADDALENA OF THE MEDICIS

Florentine family of the Italian Renaissance.

Ferdinand, [in the 1640s] delighted to be thus relieved of his distasteful conjugal duties, gave himself up to more agreeable pastimes. . . .

His other amusements were equally well known. After the birth of Cosimo, he concentrated his affections upon the person of a young count who was the handsomest of his many handsome pages. Ferdinand was too honest a man to attempt to conceal this connection from Vittoria, although he was careful, for the sake of his wife's standing, to preserve the outward aspect of a loving husband. The Tuscans, like all Italians, approved of this conduct. They could understand weaknesses of the flesh, but they could never have forgiven that debility of the spirit known as hypocrisy. Public opinion considered that Vittoria had put herself utterly in the wrong by her attitude of icy disdain after discovering Ferdinand's dalliance with the page, and from that time on, the grand duchess was hated by her subjects.

Ferdinand's mother, Grand Duchess Maddalena, was no more sympathetic than his wife. One day she burst into his chambers and, in fury, handed him a long list of prominent Florentine homosexuals. She demanded that these sinners be punished immediately, adding that their particular offence was one of especial repugnance to good Christians everywhere. Ferdinand, who himself was a sincerely devout man, took the list in silence and studied it; then he calmly took a pen and added his own name at the bottom of it.

"Don't be absurd," his mother admonished him. "You know perfectly well that you have added your name only so as to save those guilty wretches from

* This measure was first enacted by Parliament in 1533. It made homosexual acts an offence under English criminal law. With the exception of the death penalty and the forfeiture of property — both were replaced by life imprisonment in 1861 — this act remained on the Statute Book of the United Kingdom until 1967.

the punishment they deserve. I will see, all the same, that they do not escape the reward that they deserve."

"And what will that reward be, Signora?"

"The fire," the grand duchess snarled. "They must all be burned to ashes."

"Very good. It shall be as you wish." So saying, the gentle Ferdinand threw the paper into the open flames of the hearth. Then he turned again to his mother. "Behold, your sentence has already been carried out, Signora."

¶ From *The Medici: A Tale of Fifteen Generations* by James Cleugh (Garden City, N.Y.: Doubleday, 1975), pp. 334–35.

MICHEL DE MONTAIGNE (1533–1592)

French moralist and essayist.

Truly the name of brother is a beautiful name and full of affection, and for that reason he and I made our alliance a brotherhood. But that confusion of ownership, the dividing, and the fact that the richness of one is the poverty of the other, wonderfully softens and loosens the solder of brotherhood. Since brothers have to guide their careers along the same path and at the same rate, it is inevitable that they often jostle and clash with each other. Furthermore, why should the harmony and kinship which begets these true and perfect friendships be found in them? . . .

To compare this brotherly affection with affection for women, even though it is the result of our choice — it cannot be done; nor can we put the love of women in the same category. Its ardor, I confess —

Of us that goddess is not unaware
Who blends a bitter sweetness with her care

CATULLUS

— is more active, more scorching, and more intense. But it is an impetuous and fickle flame, undulating and variable, a fever flame, subject to fits and lulls, that holds us only by one corner. In friendship it is a general and universal warmth, moderate and even, besides, a constant and settled warmth, all gentleness and smoothness, with nothing bitter and stinging about it. What is more, in love there is nothing but a frantic desire for what flees from us. . . .

And that other, licentious Greek love is justly abhorred by our morality. Since it involved, moreover, according to their practice, such a necessary disparity in age and such a difference in the lovers' functions, it did not correspond closely enough with the perfect union and harmony that we require here: *For what is this love of friendship? Why does no one love either an ugly youth, or a handsome old man?* [Cicero.] For even the picture the Academy paints of it will not contradict me, I think, if I say this on the subject: that this first frenzy which the son of Venus inspired in the lover's heart at the sight of the flower of tender youth, in which they allow all the insolent and passionate acts that immoderate ardor can produce, was simply founded on external beauty, the false image of corporeal generation. For it could not be founded on the spirit, the signs of which were still hidden, which was only at its birth and before the age of budding. If this frenzy seized a base heart, the means of his courtship were riches, presents, favor in advancement to dignities, and other such base merchandise, which were generally condemned. If it fell on a nobler heart, the means were also noble: philosophical instruction, precepts to revere religion, obey the laws, die for the good of the country; examples of valor, prudence, justice; the lover studying to make himself acceptable by the grace and beauty of his soul, that of his body being long since faded, and hoping by this mental fellowship to establish a firmer and more lasting pact.

When this courtship attained its effect in due season (for whereas they do not require of the lover that he use leisure and discretion in his enterprise, they strictly require it of the loved one, because he had to judge an inner beauty, difficult to know and hidden from discovery), then there was born in the loved one the desire of spiritual conception through the medium of spiritual beauty. This was the main thing here, and corporeal beauty accidental and secondary; quite the opposite of the lover. For this reason they prefer the loved one, and prove that the gods also prefer him, and strongly rebuke the poet Aeschylus for having, in the love of Achilles and Patroclus, given the lover's part of Achilles, who was in the first beardless bloom of his youth, and the handsomest of all the Greeks.

After this general communion was established, the stronger and worthier part of it exercising its functions and predominating, they say that there resulted from it fruits very useful personally and to the public; that it constituted the strength of the countries which accepted the practice, and the principal defense of equity and liberty: witness the salutary loves of Harmodius and Aristogeiton. Therefore they call it sacred and divine. And, by their reckoning, only the violence of tyrants and the cowardice of the common people are hostile to it. In short, all that can be said in favor of the Academy is that this was a love ending in friendship; which corresponds pretty well to the Stoic definition of love: *Love is the attempt to form a friendship inspired by beauty* [Cicero].

I shall return to my description of a more equitable and more equable kind of friendship. . . .

¶ From "Of Friendship," in *The Complete Essays of Montaigne*, trans. Donald M. Frame (Stanford: Stanford University Press, 1948), pp. 136–39.

SERMON FOR INDIAN CONVERTS OF PERU

A sixteenth-century suggestion.

If there is any one among you who commits sodomy, sinning with another man, or with a boy, or with a beast, let [it] be known that, because of that, fire and brimstone fell from heaven and burned the fine cities of Sodom and Gomorrah and left them ashes.

Let it be known that it carries the death penalty under the just laws of our Spanish kings. . . .

Let it be known that the reason why God has allowed that you, the Indians, should be so affected and vexed by other nations is because of this vice that your ancestors had, and many among you still have. . . .

God will finish you, and he is already doing so if you will not reform.

Take away drunkenness and feasts which are the sowing ground of these abominable vices, remove the boys and men from your beds, do not sleep mixed up like pigs, but each one of you by himself, do not sing or say dirty words, do not entice your flesh with your hands, because this is also a sin and deserving death and hell.

¶ From the *Third Provincial Council of Lima, Peru, 1585. Cathecismo de la Doctrina Christiana Sermones*, pp. 150–54.

SAMUEL PEPYS (1633–1703)

English politician and diarist.

Upon this discourse, Sir J. Mennes and Mr. Batten both say that buggery is now almost grown as common among our gallants as in Italy, and that the very pages of the town begin to complain of their masters for it. But blessed be God, I do not to this day know what is the meaning of this sin, nor which is the agent nor which is the patient. Thence home; and my clarkes being gone by my leave to see the East India ships that are lately come home, I stayed all alone within my office all the afternoon. . . .*

¶ From *The Diary of Samuel Pepys*, vol. 4, July 1, 1663, p. 210.

---

* With the Restoration of Charles II to the British throne in 1660, there was a new tolerant attitude toward homosexual activity, with no prosecutions of any important persons over this period. Pepys wrote that the court was never as "bad" as it was during this reign, for "the most abominable vices that ever were in the world" (p. 60).

From the Enlightenment to the Nineteenth Century

BARON DE MONTESQUIEU (1689–1755)

French lawyer, philosopher, and author.

It [homosexuality] ought to be proscribed were it only for its giving to the one sex the weaknesses of the other and paving the way by a scandalous youth for an infamous old age.

¶ From *Montesquieu, The Spirit of Laws, 1748* (Berkeley: University of California Press, 1977), L. 12, chap. 6.

The crime against nature will never make any great progress in society unless people are prompted to it by some particular custom, as among the Greeks, where the youths of that country performed all their exercises naked; as amongst us, where domestic education is disused; as amongst the Asiatics, where particular persons have a great number of women whom they despise, while others can have none at all.

¶ From *Montesquieu, The Spirit of Laws, 1748* (Berkeley: University of California Press, 1977), L. 2, chap. 6.

IMMANUEL KANT (1724–1804)

German philosopher.

. . . [W]hat about a sincere commitment between two people of the same sex, the sort of homosexual equivalent of heterosexual marriage? At this point Kant invokes the notion of a *crimina carnis*, an abuse of one's sexuality. There are two kinds. First, there are acts which are contrary to sound reason, *crimina carnis secundum naturam*. These are immoral acts which go against the moral code imposed upon us as humans, and include such things as adultery. Second, there are acts contrary to our animal nature, *crimina carnis contra naturam*. These include masturbation, sex with animals, and homosexuality. They are the lowest and most disgusting sort of vice, worse in a sense even than suicide, and they are practices that we hesitate to mention. In fact, Kant found himself in something of a dilemma: mention the vices and you draw people's attention to them; fail to mention them and you do not warn people of them.

¶ From *Homosexuality: A Philosophical Inquiry* by Michael Ruse (London: Basil Blackwell, 1988), p. 185.

A second *crimen carnis contra naturam* is intercourse between sexus homogenii, in which the object of sexual impulse is a human being but there is homogeneity instead of heterogeneity of sex, as when a woman satisfies her desire on a woman, or a man on a man. This practice too is contrary to the ends of humanity; for the end of humanity in respect to sexuality is to preserve the species without debasing the person; but in this instance the species is not being preserved (as it can be by a *crimen carnis secundum naturam*), but the person is set aside, the self is degraded below the level of the animals, and humanity is dishonoured.

¶ From *Kant: Lectures on Ethics*, trans. Louis Infield (New York: Harper & Row, 1963), p. 170.

EDMUND BURKE (1729–1797)

Irish-born English statesman and author (REFLECTIONS ON THE FRENCH REVOLUTION).

The wild extravagance of his language, and of his conduct on many occasions when his passions were aroused, gave rise to reports that he was mentally unstable. It was characteristic of Burke that he should have laid himself open to the grossest charges by his imprudent zeal in taking up cases of homosexual offenders; during the Spring of 1780, in a time of national emergency, he did not hesitate to inflict upon the House of Commons an impassioned harangue on the subject of sodomy. Such instances could be multiplied, and the more Edmund was held up by his own party to the admiration of mankind as a kind of superior being, the more loud grew the whispers that this vaunted idol possessed feet of common clay.

¶ From *Edmund Burke: A Life* by Sir Philip Magnus (London: John Murray, 1939), p. 55.

In July, 1784, while Burke was wrestling with tremendous odds in his attempt to strike at Hastings in India, he was troubled by a lawsuit of an extremely unpleasant kind which he felt obliged to bring in defence of his moral character. The Press in that age was so unscrupulous that any circumstance was liable to be seized upon if it offered the chance of smirching the reputation of an opponent. Burke had inevitably provoked comment in the past by his interference on behalf of unnatural offenders, and in April, 1780, he had taken the first steps towards bringing an action for Libel against the editor of one newspaper who had accused him of sympathy with homosexual practices. On that occasion, after an apology had been tendered, Burke did not proceed with his action. He doubtless reflected that it was on the whole best to treat calumnies of that kind with contempt. Burke's interest in this matter was humanitarian, and he was anxious to obtain a slight alteration in the law. Cases had occurred in which men convicted of sodomy and placed in the pillory had been pelted to death by the mob before they were released. Burke went out of his way in the House of Commons to condemn sodomy in unequivocal terms, but he urged that those who had been convicted of practising it ought not to suffer any worse punishment than the term of imprisonment to which they had been sentenced. He contended that the pillory was not, in the circumstances, an appropriate part of the punishment which the law reserved for homosexuals, and with characteristic earnestness he endeavoured to see that the law, so long as it existed, was not enforced in that particular.

As Burke's unpopularity increased during the period of the Coalition, the old whispers against him were revived, and eventually, against the advice of his friends, a Writ for Libel was issued on Burke's behalf, against Henry Woodfall, the editor and publisher of the *Public Advertiser*. The case was tried by a Mr. Justice Buller before a Special Jury on July 14th, 1784. Burke asked for five thousand pounds from Woodfall: the Jury awarded him one hundred.

¶ From *Edmund Burke: A Life* by Sir Philip Magnus (London: John Murray, 1939), pp. 148–50.

CESARE BECCARIA (1735–1794)

Italian economist and penologist.

Pederasty, so severely punished by law and so freely subjected to tortures which triumph over innocence, is based less on man's needs when he lives in freedom and on his own, than on his passions when he lives with others in slavery. It draws its strength, not so much from a surfeit of every other pleasure, as from that education which begins by making men useless to themselves in order to make them useful to others. In those institutions packed with hot-blooded youth natural vigour, as it develops, is faced with insurmountable obstacles to every other kind of relationship and wears itself out in an activity useless to humanity, and which brings on premature old age.

¶ From *On Crimes and Punishments*, chap. 36.

THOMAS JEFFERSON (1743–1826)

Third president of the United States, drafter of THE DECLARATION OF INDEPENDENCE.

Thomas Jefferson demonstrated his liberalism by proposing [in 1777] that sodomy be punished by castration instead of death in the new penal code that would replace Virginia's Colonial charter.

¶ From *Conduct Unbecoming: Gays and Lesbians in the U.S. Military* by Randy Shilts (New York: St. Martin's, 1993), p. 12.

JEREMY BENTHAM (1748–1832)

English utilitarian philosopher, author, and law reformer.

To other subjects, it is expected that you sit down cool: but on this subject if you let it be seen that you have not sat down in a rage you have betrayed yourself at once. . . . It is a curious example to think what would have become of Socrates, and Titus, the delight of mankind, Cicero the Father of his Country . . . had they lived in these latter days. They would have perished on our gibbets. . . . I am ashamed to own that I have often hesitated whether for the sake of the interests of humanity I should expose my personal interest so much to hazard as it must be exposed to by the free discussion of a subject of this nature.

¶ From his private notes, circa 1815, quoted in "Jeremy Bentham's Essay on 'Paederasty': An Introduction" by Louis Cromptom, *Journal of Homosexuality* 3, no. 4 (Summer 1978), pp. 384–85.

To what class of offences shall we refer these irregularities of the venereal appetite which are stiled unnatural? When hidden from the public eye there could be no colour for placing them any where else: could they find a place any where it would be here. I have been tormenting myself for years to find if possible a sufficient ground for treating them with the severity with which they are treated at this time of day by all European nations: but upon the principle of utility I can find none. . . .

Whether they produce any primary mischief

1. As to any primary mischief, it is evident that it produces no pain in anyone. On the contrary it produces pleasure, and that a pleasure which, by their perverted taste, is by this supposition preferred to that pleasure which is in general reputed the greatest. The partners are both willing. If either of them be unwilling, the act is not that which we have here in view: it is an offence totally different in its nature of effects: it is a personal injury; it is a kind of rape.

As a secondary mischief whether they produce any alarm in the community

2. As to any secondary mischief, it produces not any pain of apprehension. For what is there in it for any body to be afraid of? By the supposition, those only are the objects of it who choose to be so, who find a pleasure, for so it seems they do, in being so.

Whether any danger

3. As to any danger exclusive of pain, the danger, if any, must consist in the tendency of the example. But what is the tendency of this example? To dispose others to engage in the same practises: but this practise for anything that has yet appeared produces not pain of any kind to any one.

Reasons that have commonly been assigned

Hitherto we have found no reason for punishing it at all: much less for punishing it with the degree of severity with which it has been commonly punished. . . .

What says history?

What says historical experience? The result of this can be measured only upon a large scale or upon a very general survey. Among the modern nations it is comparatively but rare. In modern Rome it is perhaps not very uncommon; in Paris probably not quite so common; in London still less frequent; in Edinburgh or Amsterdam you scarce hear of it two or three times in a century. In Athens and in antient [sic] Rome in the most flourishing periods of the history of those capitals, regular intercourse between the sexes was scarcely much more common. It was upon the same footing throughout Greece: everybody practised it; nobody was ashamed of it. They might be ashamed of what they looked upon as an excess in it, or they might be ashamed of it as a weakness, as a propensity that had a tendency to distract men from more worthy and important occupations, just as a man with us might be ashamed of excess or weakness in his love for women. . . .

It may be asked indeed, if pleasure is not a good, what is life good for, and what is the purpose of preserving it? But the most obvious and immediate consequences of a proposition may become invisible when a screen has been set before by the prejudices of false philosophy or the terrors of a false religion.

¶ From "Offences Against One's Self: Paederasty," in *Journal of Homosexuality* 3, no. 4 (Summer 1978), pp. 389–90, 392, and 4, no. 1 (Fall 1978), p. 96.

Like Kant, Bentham applied his ethical theory to homosexual behaviour. Yet although they were writing at the same time, and although Bentham's language is frequently uncomplimentary, they might as well have been in different worlds. Bentham thinks homosexual interactions as acceptable morally as Kant finds them pernicious. Such interactions give pleasure to the people engaged in them, and so by the greatest happiness principle they out to be valued. "As to any primary mischief, it is evident that [a homosexual interaction] produces no pain in anyone. On the contrary it produces pleasure. . . ."

Bentham is not advocating homosexual behaviour for everyone, only for those who want to so indulge. Then, there will be no harm. Nor is there any real problem stemming from the possibility that homosexual practices might incline or influence others into similar behaviour. People who indulge homosexual appetites seem to enjoy themselves; so at most one is inclining others to enjoyable practices.

What of the claim that homosexual behaviour runs one down physically, thus as it were reducing one's long-term pleasure in life? Bentham's conclusion is that there is no evidence to this effect. In any case, being in line with medical opinion of the time, and accepting that masturbation is physically debilitating, Bentham pointed out the injustice of trying to eliminate homosexuality through the law, when one did (and obviously could) do nothing about self-abuse.

¶ From *Homosexuality: A Philosophical Inquiry* by Michael Ruse (London: Basil Blackwell, 1988), pp. 186–87.

VOLTAIRE (FRANCOIS-MARIE AROUET) (1694–1778)

French satirist, philosopher, and historian (*CANDIDE; ZAIRE*).

How did it come about that a vice which would destroy mankind if it were general, that a sordid outrage against nature, is still so natural? It seems the highest degree of deliberate corruption, and yet it is the ordinary lot of those who have not yet had time to be corrupted. It enters hearts that are wholly inexperienced, which have not yet known ambition, fraud, or thirst for wealth; blind youth whose instincts are not sorted out throws itself into this disorder upon leaving childhood.

The inclination of the two sexes toward one another announces itself early; but whatever people have said about Africans and women of southern Asia, this inclination is generally much stronger in the man than in the woman; this is a law nature has established for all the animals. It is always the male who assaults the female.

When the young males of our species, brought up together, feel the force which nature begins to unfold in them, and fail to find the natural object of their instinct, they fall back on what resembles it. Often, for two or three years, a young man resembles a beautiful girl, with the freshness of his complexion, the brilliance of his coloring, and the sweetness of his eyes; if he is loved, it's because nature makes a mistake; homage is paid to the fair sex by attachment to one who owns its beauties, and when the years have made this resemblance disappear, the mistake ends. . . .

I cannot bear to hear people say that the Greeks authorized this license. They quote the legislator Solon, because he said in two bad verses:

Until the handsome boy must shave,
You'll cherish him and be his slave.

But really, was Solon a legislator when he wrote these two ridiculous lines? He was a youth then; but when the debauchee turned into a sage, he didn't enact such infamy into the laws of his republic. . . .

People misuse that text of Plutarch's, who in his garrulity makes one of his interlocutors say in the Dialogue on Love that women are not worthy of real love; but another interlocutor rightly upholds the women's part.

It is certain, as certain as knowledge of antiquity can be, that Socratic love was not a sordid love: this word love has deluded us. Those who were called the lovers of a young man were precisely those who are the minions of our princes today, those who were the children of honor, young men assisting in the education of a distinguished child, sharing the same studies, the same military labors: a martial and saintly institution which was wrongly turned into nocturnal feasts and orgies.

The troop of lovers established by Laius were an invincible body of young warriors bound by oath to give their lives for one another; ancient discipline never had anything finer than that.

In vain have Sextus Empiricus and others claimed that pederasty was recommended by the laws of Persia. Let them cite the text of that law; let them show the code of the Persians, and if they show it, I still shan't believe it, I shall say that the thing isn't true, because it is impossible. No, it is not in human nature to make a law that contradicts and outrages nature, a law that would annihilate mankind if it were observed to the letter. How men have taken the shameful and merely tolerated customs of a country for the laws of that country! Sextus Empiricus, who doubted everything, might well have had doubts about these statutes. If he had lived in our time, and seen two or three young Jesuits seduce some school-boys, would he have the right to say they were permitted this game by the constitutions of Ignatius de Loyola?

The love of boys was so common in Rome that they did not dare to punish this nonsense into which everyone fell heedlessly. . . . Finally, I don't believe that there has ever been a civilized nation which made laws against morals.

¶ From "Amour Nomme Socratique" ("So-Called Socratic Love"), trans. Peter Gay, in *Philosophical Dictionary* (New York: Basic Books, 1964), pp. 76–79.

JEAN-JACQUES ROUSSEAU (1712–1778)

Swiss-born French philosopher and author (THE SOCIAL CONTRACT; EMILE).

[After being nearly seduced in a Catholic hospice, the young Rousseau complained to an administrator. He wanted support; instead he was lectured against impugning a sacred place and of making much ado about nothing.]

. . . [While homosexual sex] was a forbidden act, like lechery, but yet that its intention was not to offend the person who was its object, and that I had no reason to be so vexed at having been found lovable. He told me straightforwardly that in his own youth he had the same honor, and, having been surprised in a state where he could make no resistance, he had found nothing so dreadful about it. He pushed his impudence so far as to use plain language, and, imagining that the cause of my resistance had been fear of pain, assured me that such fear was vain, and that there was nothing to be alarmed at.

¶ From *Confessions*, trans. 1783, pt. 1, bk. 2, p. 61.

SIR WILLIAM BLACKSTONE (1723–1780)

Famed English jurist.

What has been here observed, especially with regard to manner of proof, which ought to be the more clear in proportion to the crime is the more detestable, may be applied to another offence, of a still deeper malignity; the infamous crime against nature, committed either with man or beast. A crime which ought to be strictly and impartially proved, and then as strictly and impartially punished. But it is an offense of so dark a nature, so easily charged, and the negative so difficult to be proved that the accusation should be clearly made out: for, if false, it deserves a punishment inferior only to that of the crime itself.

I will not act so disagreeable a part, to my readers as well as myself, as to dwell any longer upon a subject, the very mention of which is a disgrace to human nature. It will be more eligible to imitate in this respect the delicacy of our English law, which treats it, in its very indictments, as a crime not fit to be named.

¶ From *Commentaries on the Laws of England* (Philadelphia: J.B. Lippincott, 1861), 4:215.

JOHN RUSKIN (1819–1900)

English writer and critic.

Ruskin refused to allow that it was sanctified because it was practised in ancient Athens. He argued that "the partial corruption of feeling" for women and the excessive "admiration for male physical beauty" had conduced to the fall of Greece.

¶ From *Works*, 22:235–36, 20:91.

MARY BAKER EDDY (1821–1910)

American religious leader, editor, author, and founder of Christian Science.

The formation of mortals must greatly improve to advance mankind. The scientific morale of marriage is spiritual unity. If the propagation of a higher human species is requisite to reach this goal, then its material conditions can only be permitted for the purpose of generating.

¶ From *Science and Health with Key to the Scriptures* (Boston: Trustees under the Will of Mary Baker G. Eddy, 1875), p. 62.

Man's enslavement to the most relentless masters — passion, selfishness, envy, hatred, and revenge — is conquered only by a mighty struggle. Every hour of delay makes the struggle more severe. If man is not victorious over the passions, they crush out happiness, health and manhood. Here Christian Science is the sovereign panacea, giving strength to the weakness of mortal mind — strength from the immortal and omnipotent Mind — and lifting humanity above itself into purer desires, even into spiritual power and good-will to man.

Let the slave of wrong desire learn the lessons of Christian Science, and he will get the better of that desire, and ascend a degree in the scale of human health, happiness, and existence.

¶ From *Science and Health with Key to the Scriptures* (Boston: Trustees under the Will of Mary Baker G. Eddy, 1875), p. 407.

SIR RICHARD FRANCIS BURTON (1821–1890)

English explorer, discoverer of the KAMA SUTRA, *and bringer of the* ARABIAN NIGHTS *to the West.*

He was a skilled observer, and while some officers might merely have reported that the houses [male brothels in Karachi] were indeed as rumored and were infecting the troops, Burton gave precise information. In the *Nights*, he described how boys were preferred over eunuchs because "the scrotum of the unmutilated boy could be used as a kind of bridle for directing the movements of the animal." Various of Burton's enemies, and some of his biographers, have taken for granted that he participated actively in the brothel life. There is no evidence one way or the other, and in later years, when he might have taken a "neutral" or a scholarly attitude, he was sarcastic and denigrating about "Le Vice," as he called it in the popular term of the Victorian age, and used words and phrases like analist, pathic, abuse, the evil, pathological life, "a race of born pederasts," and anus beater. Homosexuality is forbidden in the Qur'an, as Burton pointed out, and there were many instances of the most severe punishments for its practice, including death, but in Sind, Burton wrote, "Le Vice is looked upon almost as a peccadillo, and its name crops up in every jest book."

¶ From *Captain Sir Richard Francis Burton* by Edward Rice (New York: Macmillan, 1990), p. 128.

BARON RICHARD VON KRAFFT-EBING (1840–1902)

German neurologist, author of PSYCHOPATHIA SEXUALIS.

. . . [Man's sexual drive is the] most important factor in social existence, the strongest incentive to the exertion of strength and acquisition of property, to the foundation of a home, and the awakening of altruistic feeling, first for a person of the opposite sex, then for the offspring, and in a wider sense for all humanity.

Only characters endowed with strong wills are able to completely emancipate themselves from sensuality and share in that pure love from which spring the noblest joys of human life.

¶ From *Psychopathia sexualis*, trans. Charles Gilbert (1894), pp. 1, 5.

[After examining a defendant in a sodomy trial, and deciding that he could not have been guilty of homosexuality]:

> [H]e possessed neither the peculiarities of the male prostitute nor the clinical marks of effemination; and he had not the anthropological and clinical stigmata of the female-man. He was, in fact, the very opposite of this.

¶ Quoted in *The Construction of Homosexuality* by David F. Greenberg (Chicago: University of Chicago Press, 1988), p. 385.

GEORGE BERNARD SHAW (1856–1950)

Irish dramatist, critic, and social reformer (PYGMALION; MAJOR BARBARA).

[From a letter to Henry Seymour, 1898]:
The prosecution of Mr. Bedborough for selling Mr. Havelock Ellis's book [*The Psychology of Sex*] is a masterpiece of police stupidity and magisterial ignorance. . . .

My own attention was called to the subject many years ago by the passing of a sentence of twenty years' penal servitude on a harmless elderly gentleman who had been ill-advised enough to plead guilty to a piece of folly which involved no danger whatever to society. At that time I was as ignorant as most people are on the subject; but the sentence so shocked my common humanity that I made an attempt to get the press to protest. I then discovered that the fear of becoming suspected of personal reasons for desiring a change in the law in this matter, makes every Englishman an abject coward, truckling to the vilest vulgar superstitions, and professing in public and in print views which have not the slightest resemblance to those which he expresses in private conversation with educated and thoughtful men. This hypocrisy is much more degrading to the public than the subject of Mr. Havelock Ellis's book can possibly be, because it is universal instead of being accidental and peculiar. In Germany and France the free circulation of such works as the one of Mr. Havelock Ellis's now in question has done a good deal to make the public in those countries understand that decency and sympathy are as necessary in dealing with sexual as with any other subjects. In England we still repudiate decency and sympathy and make virtues of blackguards and ferocity.

¶ From *Bernard Shaw: Collected Letters, 1898–1910*, ed. Dan H. Laurence (London: Max Reinhardt, 1972), pp. 57–58.

[From a letter to the Dean of Windsor, 1928]:
My own experience of life has led me — as a matter of necessary practice — to treat sexual life as outside the scope of the judgments we have to pass on one another for social, political, and business purposes. I have not found that even the most absurd aberrations are necessarily associated with any general depravity of character, or that intemperance in their practice has any other results than the intemperance in normal sexual intercourse which visibly damages many respectably married persons. I should say that a dishonoured cheque is a safer index to character for worldly purposes than inversion. But this is only a rule of thumb; for the impossibility of getting at the facts on any statistical scale puts anything like a scientific generalisation out of the question. I have all the normal repugnances to aberrations; but I have found that they are untrustworthy guides in estimating character. Normally sexed people are sometimes as devoid of conscience as it is humanly possible to be: homosexualists are sometimes conspicuously able and highminded. Denunciations of homosexuality as depraving and detestable may have an unsuspected and deeply wounding effect on one's most justly valued friends. The wisest and best inverts never tell; but they can cherish a deep grudge against those who would, if they knew, turn against them, and attribute to them general vices of which they are conspicuously innocent.

¶ From *Bernard Shaw: Collected Letters, 1926–1950*, ed. Dan H. Lawrence (London: Max Reinhardt, 1988), p. 119.

THE BOOK OF MORMON OF THE CHURCH OF JESUS CHRIST OF LATTER-DAY SAINTS, 1879

For Jerusalem is ruined, and Judah is fallen, because their tongues and their doings have been against the Lord, to provoke the eyes of his glory.

The show of their countenance doth witness against them, and doth declare their sin to be even as Sodom, and they cannot hide it. Wo unto their souls, for they have rewarded evil unto themselves!

¶ From 2 Nephi 13:8–9.

WILLIAM ACTON (1813–1875)

British medical writer (THE FUNCTIONS AND DISORDERS OF THE REPRODUCTIVE ORGANS).

[On the consequences of masturbation]:
The frame is stunted and weak, the muscles undeveloped, the eye is sunken and heavy, the complexion is sallow, pasty, or covered with spots of acne, the hands are damp and cold, and the skin moist. The boy shuns the society of others, creeps about alone, joins with repugnance in the amusements of his schoolfellows. He cannot look anyone in the face, and becomes careless in dress and uncleanly in person. His intellect has become sluggish and enfeebled, and if his habits are persisted in, he may end in becoming a drivelling idiot or a peevish valetudinarian. Such boys are to be seen in all stages of degeneration, but what we have described is but the result towards which they all are tending.

. . . [It threatens the virility] necessary to give a man that consciousness of dignity, of his character as head and ruler, and of his importance, which is absolutely essential to the well-being of the family, and through it, of society itself.

¶ From *The Functions and Disorders of the Reproductive Organs*, 1857.

THE STATE OF INDIANA'S FIRST SODOMY LAW, 1881

Whoever commits the abominable and detestable crime against nature by having carnal knowledge with mankind or beast; or who, being a male, carnally knows any man or woman through the anus; and whoever entices, allures, instigates or aids any person under the age of twenty-one to commit masturbation or self-pollution is guilty of sodomy, and upon conviction thereof, shall be imprisoned in the State prison not more than fourteen nor less than two years.

¶ Quoted in *The Construction of Homosexuality* by David F. Greenberg (Chicago: University of Chicago Press, 1988), p. 401.

GEORGE BEARD (1839–1883)

Prominent nineteenth-century U.S. doctor.

. . . [T]he sex is perverted, they hate the opposite sex, and love their own; men become women, and women men, in their tastes, conduct, character, feelings, and behavior.

¶ From *Sexual Neurasthenia* (New York: E.B. Treat, 1884), p. 107.

SIGMUND FREUD (1856–1939)

Austrian neurologist, the originator of psychoananalysis.

There comes a time in the development of the individual at which he unifies his sexual instincts (which have hitherto been engaged in auto-erotic activities) in order to obtain a love-object; and he begins by taking himself, his own body, as his love-object; and only subsequently proceeds from this to the choice of some person other than himself as his object. This half-way phase between auto-eroticism and object-love may perhaps be indispensable to the normal course of life; but it appears that many people linger unusually long in this condition, and that many of its features are carried over by them into the later stages of their development. The point of central interest in the self which is thus chosen as a love-object may already be the genitals. The line of development then leads on to the choice of an outer object with similar genitals — that is, to homosexual object-choice — and thence to heterosexuality. Persons who are manifest homosexuals in later life have, it may be presumed, never emancipated themselves from the binding condition that the object of their choice must possess genitals like their own. . . .

¶ From *The Complete Psychological Works of Sigmund Freud* (London: Hogarth, 1911), 12:81–82.

I am . . . of the firm conviction that homosexuals must not be treated as sick people, for a perverse orientation is far from being a sickness. Would that not oblige us to characterize as sick many great thinkers and scholars of all times, whose perverse orientation we know for a fact and whom we admire precisely because of their mental health? Homosexual persons are not sick.

¶ From *Die Zeit*, October 27, 1903.

It is not for psychoanalysis to solve the problem of homosexuality. It must rest content with discovering the psychical mechanisms that resulted in determination of the object-choice, and with tracing the paths leading from them to the instinctual basis of the disposition. There its work ends, and it leaves the rest to biological research.

¶ From *The Psychogenesis of a Case of Homosexuality in a Woman*, 1920.

Your query, dear Ernest, concerning prospective membership of homosexuals has been considered by us [Freud and Otto Rank] and we disagree with you. In effect we cannot exclude such persons without other sufficient reasons, as we cannot agree with their legal prosecution. We feel that a decision in such cases should depend upon a thorough examination of the other qualities of the candidate.

¶ From *Beyond the Pleasure Principle*, 1921.

Dear Mrs. ______,
I gather from your letter that your son is a homosexual. I am most impressed by the fact that you do not mention this term yourself in your information about him. May I question you, why you avoid it? Homosexuality is assuredly no advantage, but it is nothing to be ashamed of, no vice, no degradation, it cannot be classified as an illness; we consider it to be a variation of the sexual function produced by a certain arrest of sexual development.

Many highly respectable individuals of ancient and modern times have been homosexuals, several of the greatest men among them (Plato, Michelangelo, Leonardo da Vinci, etc.). It is a great injustice to persecute homosexuality as a crime, and cruelty too. If you do not believe me, read the books of Havelock Ellis.

By asking me if I can help, you mean, I suppose, if I can abolish homosexuality and make normal heterosexuality take its place. The answer is, in a general way, we cannot promise to achieve it. In a certain number of cases we succeed in developing the blighted germs of heterosexual tendencies which are present in every homosexual, in the majority of cases it is no more possible. It is a question of the quality and the age of the individual. The result of treatment cannot be predicted.

What analysis can do for your son runs in a different line. If he is unhappy, neurotic, torn by conflicts, inhibited in his social life, analysis may bring him harmony, peace of mind, full efficiency, whether he remains a homosexual or gets changed.

If you make up your mind he should have analysis with me (I don't expect you will!!), he has to come over to Vienna. I have no intention of leaving here. However, don't neglect to give me your answer.

Sincerely yours with kind wishes,

FREUD

¶ Quoted in *The Life and Work of Sigmund Freud* by Ernest Jones, ed. and abr. Lionel Trilling and Steven Marcus (Garden City, N.Y.: Anchor Books, 1963), p. 490.

PAUL CLAUDEL (1868–1955)

French dramatist and poet.

The line between acceptable and bad, deviant sex must be the possibility of issue. Otherwise where do you draw the line? If one pretends to justify sodomy, another will justify onanism, vampirism, rape of children, cannibalism, etc. There is no reason to stop.

¶ From a letter to [the gay novelist] André Gide, 1914.

EMMA GOLDMAN (1869–1940)

American feminist and revolutionary.

. . . [S]he stressed the power of the sexual impulse over all aspects of life and argued that sexual repression not only harmed health but inhibited intellectual and artistic creativity as well. Beginning in 1895 with her defense of Oscar Wilde during his trial, Goldman extended the basic anarchist idea of "noninvasion" to a defense of homosexuality. In what may have been her most audacious lecture, "Vice" (later she would draw on the work of Edward Carpenter to discuss "The Intermediate Sex"), she insisted that sex was an absolutely private affair into which state, church, or other people had no right to intrude. She argued that any act entered into voluntarily by two people was not vice. "What is usually hastily condemned as vice by thoughtless individuals, such as homosexuality, masturbation, etc.," she advised, "should be considered from a scientific viewpoint, and not in a moralizing way."

For Emma, "the sex question" was also emphatically a woman's question, since women suffered most from repressive sexual values.

¶ From *Emma Goldman: An Intimate Life* by Alice Wexler (New York: Random House, 1984), p. 94.

From the Turn of the Twentieth Century to World War II

LORD BADEN-POWELL OF GILWELL (1857–1941)

Founder of the Boy Scout movement.

Smoking and drinking are things that tempt some fellows and not others, but there is one temptation that is pretty sure to come to you at one time or another, and I want just to warn you against it.

You would probably be surprised if you knew how many boys have written to me thanking me for what I have written on this subject, so I expect there are more who will be glad of a word of advice against the secret vice which gets hold of so many fellows. Smoking and drinking and gambling are men's vices and therefore attract some boys, but this secret vice is not a man's vice — men have nothing but contempt for a fellow who gives way to it.

Some boys, like those who start smoking, think it is a very fine and manly thing to tell or listen to dirty stories, but it only shows them to be little fools.

Yet such talk and the reading of trashy books or looking at lewd pictures are very apt to lead a thoughtless boy into the temptation of self-abuse. This is a most dangerous thing for him, for, should it become a habit, it tends to lower both health and spirits.

But if you have any manliness in you, you will throw off such temptation at once. You will stop looking at the books and listening to the stories, and will give yourself something else to think about.

Sometimes the desire is brought on by indigestion, or from eating too rich food, or from constipation or from sleeping in too warm a bed with too many blankets. It can therefore be cured by correcting these, and by bathing at once in cold water, or by exercising the upper part of the body by arm exercises, boxing, etc.

It may seem difficult to overcome the temptation the first time, but when you have done so once it will be easier afterwards.

If you still have trouble about it, do not make a secret of it, but go to your father, or your Scoutmaster, and talk it over with him, and all will come right.

¶ From *Scouting for Boys: A Handbook for Instruction in Good Citizenship Through Woodcraft* (Boy Scouts of America, 1915), pp. 225–27.

HAVELOCK ELLIS (1859–1939)

English psychologist, essayist, and art critic.

Sexual Inversion was an unprecedented book. Never before had homosexuality been treated so soberly, so comprehensively, so sympathetically. To read it today is to read the voice of common sense and compassion; to read it then [it was published in 1897] was, for the great majority, to be affronted by a deliberate incitement to vice of the most degrading kind.

Ellis's aim was to dispel myth, to puncture prejudice, and to present as factual a report of the real situation as possible. The first sentence of the book marks his consistent view of the subject: "Sexual inversion, as here understood, means sexual instinct turned by inborn constitutional abnormality toward persons of the same sex." Ellis was not the first to proclaim the organic nature of inversion, but he was the first person to write a book in English which treated homosexuality as neither a disease nor a crime. That such sexual proclivity is not determined by suggestion, accident or historical conditioning is apparent, he argues, from the fact that it is widespread among animals and that there is abundant evidence of its prevalence among various nations at all periods of history. The incidence of relatives sharing the same propensities, Ellis also sees as firm evidence of the inherited character of inversion. Ellis rejects Ulrichs's theory of an invert as a man in whom a female soul is imprisoned; but he does take pains to emphasize the artistic inclinations of a large portion of his subjects and their tendency to "Neurasthenia" — that vague nineteenth-century word covering a wide spectrum of nervous ailments. Most people regarded homosexuality (a word rejected by Ellis because it could cover experiences arising out of temporary circumstances) as manifestations of the criminal or the insane, but Ellis stresses that none of his cases has been charged with a misdemeanour (although many had contemplated suicide) nor are they degenerates, but are frequently found among the most cultivated members of the community. Famous inverts include Erasmus, Leonardo, Michelangelo, Cellini, Sappho — most of them non-English, it is true. He decided to omit Shakespeare's name, as this might prove too outrageous for English readers to swallow.

The persuasiveness of his argument is based on his thirty-three case-histories. . . .

Freud was later to object that Ellis avoided "decisions" — that is, committing himself to certain positions (perhaps the Freudian!) about the dynamics of the psyche. But in this book he spoke out more clearly, more directly, more responsibly than he was ever to do again. "When I review the cases I have brought forward," he concluded, "and the mental history of inverts I have known, I am inclined to say that if we can enable an invert to be healthy, self-restrained and self-respecting, we have often done better than to convert him into the mere feeble simulacrum of a normal man." From his pages the invert emerges as a mutation, an anomaly, a "sport," to be compared perhaps with those who possess colour-hearing, which, after all, may be regarded as a sort of talent, so that it is possible to assume that the invert is not only an acceptable member of society but a talented one. . . .

¶ From *Havelock Ellis: A Biography* by Phyllis Grosskurth (Toronto: McClelland & Stewart, 1980), pp. 185–86, 189–90.

The fact that homosexuality is especially common among men of exceptional talent was long since noted by Dante. [He quotes here from *The Inferno*]. It has been noted since and remains a remarkable fact.

There cannot be the slightest doubt that intellectual and artistic abilities of the highest order have frequently been associated with a congenitally inverted sexual temperment.

¶ From *Studies in the Psychology of Sex* (Philadelphia: F.A. Davis, 1928), 2:26.

Inversion is as likely to be accompanied by high intellectual ability in a woman as a man.

¶ From *Studies in the Psychology of Sex* (Philadelphia: F.A. Davis, 1928), 2:196.

SIR WINSTON CHURCHILL (1874–1965)

English statesman and author (HISTORY OF THE ENGLISH-SPEAKING PEOPLES; THE SECOND WORLD WAR).

Winston Churchill once barked to a British admiral lecturing him on naval tradition, "Don't talk to me about naval tradition. It's nothing but rum, sodomy, and the lash."

¶ From *Conduct Unbecoming: Gays and Lesbians in the U.S. Military* by Randy Shilts (New York: St. Martin's, 1993), p. 401.

Back in London in October [1906], he found himself embroiled once more in the coolie question. . . . Churchill's policy of voluntary repatriation had been approved on May 1. Proclamations in Chinese were posted in the mines, promising repatriation to any coolie who could give half of one month's wages toward the trip home. . . .

Hardly a day went by in the House without a question about the coolies. Inquiries had shifted from the injustice of their contracts to their unruly behavior. The coolies seemed to have brought with them every social evil. They gambled and started riots. . . .

Equally shocking to the turn-of-the-century English mind was the crime of homosexuality. In August, Churchill had been asked to comment on reports that the Chinese, deprived of their families, were practicing unnatural vices on a large scale. A Cape Colony solicitor named Leopold Luyt had written several MP's that homosexuality in the compounds was open and scandalous. . . .

Churchill pledged that an inquiry would be made at once. . . .

Here was the Empire, that brotherhood of nations linked by a common code of honor, fostering the most reprehensible kind of vice. A great moral disaster was being hushed up. . . . Had the prevalence of this vice long been known to the mine inspectors, who would do nothing about it? What a taint on South Africa!

Churchill had to maintain the confidentiality of the report while pacifying the House. . . .

What was true, Churchill went on, was "that this particular offense of sodomy prevailed in most if not all compounds . . . and that there were in these compounds persons who lent themselves to these practices either from habit or for money who were, in fact, proved to be catamites." . . .

The important thing, Churchill said, was that "the revelations of Mr. Bucknill's report disclosed a sufficiently unhealthy, unwholesome, and unnatural condition of affairs to seal the fate of Chinese labor . . . the system must absolutely, totally, utterly come to a close."

The speech was a great success. Pleased with himself, Churchill told Eddie Marsh, "I smote the Radicals hip and thigh from Sodom and Gomorrha." He also broke new linguistic ground. The word "catamite" had never been used in the House before. Eddie wrote a friend that it was a great puzzle to the MP's; hardly anyone knew that it was just a fancy name for a bugger.

¶ From *Churchill: Young Man in a Hurry, 1874–1915* by Ted Morgan (New York: Simon & Schuster, 1982), pp. 200–03.

SIDONIE GABRIELLE COLETTE (1873–1954)

French novelist.

Up to now were they [gay men] ever observed by any woman for the length of time they were observed by me? Ordinarily women — and let's say an ordinary woman — tries to entice a homosexual. Naturally she fails. She then decides she despises them. Or else — and the case is not rare — she wins a physical victory which gives her cause for pride: she has achieved a kind of brilliant advantage over him, but futile and misleading because she gives an exaggerated importance to external signs.

¶ From *Pure and Impure* (New York: Farrar, Straus, and Giroux, 1966), 141–42.

D.H. LAWRENCE (1885–1930)

English author (SONS AND LOVERS; WOMEN IN LOVE; LADY CHATTERLEY'S LOVER).

[From a letter to philosopher Bertrand Russell on February 12, 1915]: The ordinary Englishman of the educated class goes to a woman now to masterbate [sic] himself. Because he is not going for discovery or new connection or progression, but only to repeat upon himself a known reaction. When this condition arrives, there is always Sodomy.

¶ From *Collected Letters*, ed. Harry T. Moore (New York: Viking, 1962), p. 285.

[The sex organ and the excrementory functions] work so close together, yet they are, so to speak, utterly different in direction. Sex is a creative flow, the excrementory flow is towards dissolution, de-creation. . . . In the really healthy human being the distinction between the two is instant, our profoundest instincts are perhaps our instincts of opposition between the two flows.

But in the degraded human being the deep instincts have gone dead, and the two flows become identical.

[Masturbation is] perhaps the deepest and most dangerous cancer of our civilization. . . . certainly the most dangerous sexual vice that a society can be afflicted with, in the long run.

¶ From *Pornography and Obscenity, An Essay* by D.H. Lawrence (Yonkers, N.Y.: Alicat Book Shop, 1948), pp. 313–14, 317.

CARL JUNG (1875–1961)

Swiss psychiatrist.

I asked myself whether the growing masculination of the white woman is not connected with the loss of her natural wholeness . . . ; whether it is not a compensation for her impoverishment; and whether the feminizing of the white man is not a further consequence. The more rational the polity, the more blurred is the difference between the sexes. The role homosexuality plays in modern society is enormous. It is partly the consequence of the mother-complex, partly a purposive phenomenon (prevention of reproduction).

¶ From *Memories, Dreams, Reflections,* ed. Aniela Jaffe, trans. Richard and Clara Winston (New York: Random House, 1963), pp. 263–64.

If we regard sexuality as consisting of a fixed heterosexual and a fixed homosexual component we shall never explain this case [involving a young man who had been homosexual in adolescence, heterosexual in early adulthood, and later again homosexual], since the assumption of fixed components precludes any kind of transformation. . . . [W]e must assume a great mobility of the sexual components. . . .

¶ From *Collected Works,* ed. Herbert Read, Michael Fordham, and Gerhard Adler (New York: Pantheon Books, 1953–1979), 4:109.

It follows that Jung will be more likely to credit the possibility of "curing" homosexuality than Freud, and will also tend to see "cure" as desirable. Because Jung believes that mature sexuality will be contrasexual, he sees redirecting homosexually oriented sexuality into a heterosexual path as a matter of education, of helping the psyche move forward in its natural direction.

¶ From *Myths and Mysteries of Same-Sex Love* by Christine Downing (New York: Continuum, 1989), p. 111.

In view of the recognized frequency of this phenomenon [homosexuality], its interpretation as a pathological perversion is very dubious. The psychological findings show that it is rather a matter of incomplete detachment from the hermaphroditic archetype, coupled with a distinct resistance to identify with the role of a one-sided sexual being. Such a disposition should not be adjudged negative in all circumstances, in so far as it preserves the archetype of the Original Man, which a one-sided sexual being has, up to a point, lost.

¶ From *Collected Works*, ed. Herbert Read, Michael Fordham, and Gerhard Adler (New York: Pantheon Books, 1953–1979), 9i:71.

Since a "mother-complex" is a concept borrowed from psychopathology, it is always associated with the idea of injury and illness. But if we take the concept out of its narrow psychopathological setting and give it a wider connotation, we can see that it has positive effects as well.

Thus a man with a mother-complex may have a finely differentiated Eros instead of, or in addition to, homosexuality (something of this sort is suggested by Plato in his Symposium). This gives him a great capacity for friendship, which often creates ties of astonishing tenderness between men and may even rescue friendship between the sexes from the limbo of the impossible. He may have good taste and an aesthetic sense which are fostered by the presence of a feminine streak. Then he may be supremely gifted as a teacher because of his almost feminine insight and tact. He is likely to have a feeling for history, and to be conservative in the best sense and cherish the values of the past. Often he is endowed with a wealth of religious feelings, which help to bring the *ecclesia spiritualis* into reality; and a spiritual receptivity which makes him responsive to revelation.

¶ From *Collected Works*, ed. Herbert Read, Michael Fordham, and Gerhard Adler (New York: Pantheon Books, 1953–1979), 9i:86–87.

But only too often this condition ["ideal homosexuality"] is lacking. The more homosexual a man is, the more prone he is to disloyalty and to the seduction of boys. Even when loyalty and true friendship prevail the results may be undesirable for the development of personality. A friendship of this kind naturally involves a special cult of feeling, of the feminine element in a man. He becomes gushing, soulful, aesthetic, over-sensitive, etc. — in a word, effeminate, and this womanish-behavior is detrimental to his character.

¶ From *Collected Works*, ed. Herbert Read, Michael Fordham, and Gerhard Adler (New York: Pantheon Books, 1953–1979), 10:107.

JOHN JAY CHAPMAN (1862–1933)

American essayist and author.

[On discovering that the Greek mind was "abnormal"]:
But why had I not found this out before? Because the books and essays on Plato which I had been reading were either accommodated to the Greek psychology or else they were accommodated to modern Miss Nancyism — and, by the way, the two agree very sociably.

[On the passing on of Greek vices across Europe]:
They spread like fungi that survive in the depth of a tangled forest.

¶ From *Lucian, Plato and Greek Morals* (Boston: Houghton Mifflin, 1931), p. 120.

WYNDHAM LEWIS (1882–1957)

British novelist (THE APES OF GOD; THE HUMAN AGE), essayist, and painter.

But if you have set out to give an "intellectual" a dose of hate-poison, to get him into the required destructive fever, you cannot achieve this by the same methods that you would employ with an unskilled labourer or a street hawker. . . .

All the processes of this intellectualist stimulation to "revolt" are essentially and from the start *unreal.*

Some habit, such as a drug-habit, is exceedingly useful, as might be expected. For that impairs the stability and independence of the individual in question and *separates* him, somewhat, from other men — *the vulgar herd that does not drug.* Then homosexuality may also be made to serve this purpose of *separation,* and that of a self-destructive hostility. This separatist psychology of the homosexual has been excellently described by Proust — the intense "outcast" *esprit de corps* of the born pathic — but this is merely a very rough-and-ready indication of the methods suitable for jockeying an up-till-then member of some normal majority into the minority-position of defensive hostility, and subsequently of universal hatred, which is needed for Apocalypse, of the more drastic civil sort.

¶ From "Hatred as prescribed for the 'Intellectual' and as prescribed for the Mob," in *The Diabolical Principle* (London: Chatto and Windus, 1931), pp. 78–80.

FRANTZ FANON (1925–1961)

*Sociologist and author (*BLACK SKIN, WHITE MASKS*).*

The Negrophobic woman is in fact nothing but a putative sexual partner — just as the Negrophobic man is a repressed homosexual.

There are, for instance, men who go to "houses" in order to be beaten by negroes; passive homosexuals who insist on black partners.

I have never been able, without revulsion, to hear a *man* say of another man: "He is so sensual!" I do not know what the sensuality of a man is. Imagine a woman saying of another woman: She's so terribly desirable — she's darling.

[Homosexuality is] the white man's disease.

¶ From *Black Skin, White Masks*, trans. Charles Lam Markmann (New York: Grove, 1967), pp. 156, 180.

DYLAN THOMAS (1914–1953)

Welsh poet.

[From a letter to Pamela Hansford Johnson on December 21, 1933]:
Have you remarked upon the terrible young men of this generation, the willing-buttocked, celluloid-trousered, degenerates who are gradually taking the place of the bright young things of even five years ago? Or is the degeneracy, the almost unbelievable effeminacy, the product of the Welsh slums alone? In an hotel last night a boy, wearing a light green hat, white shirt, red tie, light green trousers and tightly fitting fawn overcoat, went up to the bar and said "A whate and a smale Ardathe, girlie." I heard him. He was the most perfect example I've ever seen, the sort of thing one hears of in coarse stories but rarely encounters in the flesh (God deliver me from the flesh; the outer trappings are enough). I see more and more of them every day. They always existed, but in recent months — it seems months to me — they are coming, unashamedly, out into the open. I saw one with a drunken nigger last night.

It is the only vice, I think, that revolts me and makes me misanthropic. I can — theoretically — tolerate incest . . . and other domestic sins. But the sin of the boy with the nigger goes up like a rocketed scab to heaven.

¶ From *Collected Letters of Dylan Thomas*, ed. Paul Ferris (Toronto: Fitzhenry & Whiteside, 1985), p. 71.

ANNA FREUD (1895–1982)

Psychoanalyst, pioneer in child studies.

[From a lecture on homosexuality]:
. . . [T]he active male partner, whom these men were seeking, represents to them their lost masculinity, which they enjoy in identification with him. This implies that these apparently passive men are active according to their fantasy, while they are passive only so far as their behavior is concerned.

. . . [N]arcissistically they loved their own genital, just as in childhood they had wanted someone [usually the mother] to admire it or to share their own admiration of it with them.

Such persons [homosexuals and impotent males] see the relation to a love object exclusively in passive terms. To love means: to be maltreated, kicked about, impoverished, tormented, possessed. . . . Paradoxically, then, for these patients the symptom of impotence in intercourse serves the preservation of their masculinity.

[In 1956, Anna Freud recommended to a journalist that the latter not quote from her father Sigmund's favorable 1935 letter about homosexuality, and explained why]:

> There are several reasons for this, one being that nowadays we can cure many more homosexuals than was thought possible in the beginning. The other reason is that readers may take this as a confirmation that all that analysis can do is to convince patients that their defects or "immoralities" do not matter and that they should be happy with them. That would be unfortunate.

¶ Quoted in *Anna Freud: A Biography* by Elisabeth Young-Bruehl (New York: Summit Books, 1988), pp. 325–26, 327.

ADOLF HITLER (1889–1945)

Leader of Nazi Germany (1933–1945).

Organizational considerations were, however, not the only factors shaping Nazi policy toward homosexuality: a party statement issued in May 1938 condemned it in the name of masculinity, might, and discipline. Yet in practice, homosexuality within party ranks was tolerated, and Hitler even defended [Ernst] Röhm against charges of homosexuality, saying it was his own private affair. . . . In any event, in the early 1930s, Hitler reversed his policy of toleration. Within a month of his appointment as chancellor of Germany in January 1933, the government banned homosexual-rights organizations. Later in the same year it instigated raids on gay bars and sponsored the vandalizing of Magnus Hirschfeld's Institute of Sexual Science. The following year it had Röhm shot. These steps were taken when it became necessary to present an image of respectability to the middle class whose political support Hitler was trying to win. The contrast between the image of sexual purity projected by the Nazis and the decadence of Weimar Berlin's nightlife, where male and female homosexuality were highly visible, may have gained the Nazis some support.

¶ From *The Construction of Homosexuality* by David F. Greenberg (Chicago: University of Chicago Press, 1988), pp. 438 n. 14.

NAZI PARTY OF GERMANY

Statement made when still in opposition.

[Nazi Party statement on homosexuality, made in response to a question about its stance toward reform [i.e., softening] of Paragraph 175, the anti-homosexuality law of the Second Reich]:

It is not necessary that you and I live, but it is necessary that the German people live. And it can only live if it can fight, for life means fighting. And it can only fight if it maintains its masculinity. It can only maintain its masculinity if it exercises discipline, especially in matters of love. Free love and deviance are undisciplined. Therefore, we reject you, as we reject anything that hurts our nation.

Anyone who thinks of homosexual love is our enemy. We reject anything which emasculates our people and makes it a plaything for our enemies, for we know that life is a fight, and it is madness to think that men will ever embrace fraternally. Natural history teaches us the opposite. Might makes right. The strong will always win over the weak. Let us see to it that we once again become the strong! But this we can achieve only in one way — the German people must once again learn how to exercise discipline. We therefore reject any form of lewdness, especially homosexuality, because it robs us of our last chance to free our people from the bondage which now enslaves it.

¶ Published on May 14, 1928, quoted in *The Pink Triangle: The Nazi War against Homosexuals* by Richard Plant (New York: Henry Holt, 1986), p. 50.

NAZI GERMANY

[Paragraph 175 of the Prussian Penal Code was adopted for the new Second Reich by Kaiser Wilhelm I of Germany in 1871, making sexual acts between males punishable. Over the next six decades, however, most German courts prosecuted only homosexual behavior which resembled "coital acts."

On January 28, 1935, the still-young National Socialist regime of Adolf Hitler added several amendments to the earlier law.]

175:

1. A male who indulges in criminally indecent activities with another male or who allows himself to participate in such activities will be punished with jail.
2. If one of the participants is under the age of twenty-one, and if the crime has not been grave, the court may dispense with the jail sentence.

175(a): A jail sentence of up to ten years or, if mitigating circumstances can be established, a jail sentence of no less than three years will be imposed on

1. any male who by force or by threat of violence and danger to life and limb compels another man to indulge in criminally indecent activities, or allows himself to participate in such activities;
2. any male who forces another male to indulge with him in criminally indecent activities by using the subordinate position of the other man, whether it be at work or elsewhere, or who allows himself to participate in such activities;

3. any male who indulges professionally and for profit in criminally indecent activities with other males, or allows himself to be used for such activities or who offers himself for same.

175(b): Criminally indecent activities by males with animals are to be punished by jail; in addition, the court may deprive the subject of his civil rights.

¶ From *The Pink Triangle: The Nazi War against Homosexuals* by Richard Plant (New York: Henry Holt, 1986), p. 206.

HEINRICH HIMMLER (1900–1945)

A founder of the Nazi Party, organizer of the SS *and Gestapo.*

[Himmler] announced that there could be no homosexual men in the state service because they would tend to award positions to one another instead of on merit. From that time on, any SS member convicted of homosexuality was executed. Women were to be kept out for the same reason, though lesbianism did not pose a comparable threat to Nazi goals and was never even made criminal.

Like many of his era whose fear of homosexuality reached paranoid proportions, Himmler believed that homosexuals could recognize one another, making it possible for them to aid or conspire with even secret homosexuals and bring down the *Männerstaat.*

¶ From *The Construction of Homosexuality* by David F. Greenberg (Chicago: University of Chicago Press, 1988), p. 438 n. 13.

[From a speech given on October 11, 1936, following the murder of the homosexual Nazi leader Ernst Röhm and others, during the Blood Purge]: [W]e did not hesitate to strike this plague with death, even within our own ranks.

Just as we today have gone back to the ancient Germanic view on the question of marriage mixing different races, so too in our judgment of homosexuality — a symptom of degeneracy which could destroy our race — we must return to the guiding Nordic principle: extermination of degenerates.

¶ From *The Nazi Extermination of Homosexuals* by Frank Rector (New York: Stein & Day, 1981), p. 122.

[From a speech made in 1937]:
It would be a catastrophe if we foolish males wanted to make women into logically thinking instruments. . . . [I]f we try to masculinize them, well, there we conjure up the danger of homosexuality. . . .

If a man just looks at a girl in America, he can be forced to marry her or pay damages . . . therefore men protect themselves in the U.S.A. by turning to homosexuals. . . . [W]omen in the U.S.A. are like battle-axes — they hack away at males. . . .

An adolescent male must be encouraged to fall in love with a girl of good blood; then he will turn away from homosexuals, will not participate in juvenile orgies of a homosexual nature. . . .

If we don't encourage this correct heterosexual behavior, we will have sexually disturbed youngsters, not the right material for the elite SS, the new Holy Order. It is essential for a nation to guide sex in the right direction.

¶ Quoted in *The Pink Triangle: The Nazi War against Homosexuals* by Richard Plant (New York: Henry Holt, 1986), pp. 91–92.

[In response to an urging not to have homosexuals murdered]:
I can tell you why. . . . It's because we mean to get rid of homosexuals root and branch. They're a danger to the national health. Just think how many children will never be born because of this, and how a people can be broken in nerve and spirit when such a plague gets hold of it.

If a man has an affair with his pretty secretary, at most she will exert some influence over him, but she won't affect his ability to work. In certain circumstances there will be a child. But when a man in the Security Service, in the SS or in the Government has homosexual tendencies, then he abandons the normal order of things for the perverted world of the homosexuals. Such a man always drags ten others after him, otherwise he can't survive. We can't permit such a danger to the country; the homosexuals must be entirely eliminated. . . . The homosexual is a traitor to his own people and must be rooted out.

¶ From *The Nazi Extermination of Homosexuals* by Frank Rector (New York: Stein & Day, 1981), p. 123.

[In a 1937 order, retroactively applied, when asked if the homosexual may have fathered children]:
So much the worse. For then the homosexual tendency will be inherited.

After serving the sentence imposed by the court, they [SS and any police officers who had been arrested for homosexual acts] will, upon my instructions, be taken to a concentration camp and there shot while attempting to escape.

¶ From *The Nazi Extermination of Homosexuals* by Frank Rector (New York: Stein & Day, 1981), p. 123.

[From a circular sent by Himmler to all SS and police units, following the announcement on November 15, 1941, of a decree laying down the death penalty for any member of the SS or police who engaged in sex with another male]:

1. In order to keep the SS and police free from homosexually inclined weaklings, the Fuhrer has ruled that any member of the SS or police who engages in indecent behavior with another man or permits himself to be abused by him for indecent purposes will, regardless of age, be condemned to death and executed. In less grave cases, a term of not less than six years' penal servitude or imprisonment may be imposed.
2. The Fuhrer's decree will not be published because it might give rise to misinterpretation.

¶ From *The Nazi Extermination of Homosexuals* by Frank Rector (New York: Stein & Day, 1981), p. 123.

PAUL JOSEPH GOEBBELS (1897–1945)

Nazi propaganda minister.

[Upon hearing of the November 15, 1941, decree by Himmler, laying down the death penalty for SS and police officers who engage in homosexual relations with other males]:
An extremely beneficial decree, and one which will preserve the elite organization from this cancerous disease.

¶ Diary entry of November 1941, quoted in *The Nazi Extermination of Homosexuals* by Frank Rector (New York: Stein & Day, 1981), p. 123.

DR. ALFRED KINSEY (1894–1956)

Zoologist, author of SEXUAL BEHAVIOR IN THE HUMAN MALE.

[From a letter to a male homosexual youth]:
Do not be discouraged if you find the male still arousing you more than the female; it may take time and abundant heterosexual experience to bring you satisfaction equal to what you have known in the homosexual. Sometimes, however, I have known the homosexual pattern to change almost overnight, as the result of a fortunately satisfactory heterosexual experience.

¶ From *Dr. Kinsey and the Institute for Sex Research* by Wardell B. Pomeroy (New York: Harper & Row, 1972), p. 77.

[To a doctor in New Wilmington, Pennsylvania]:
We are not particularly interested in any sexual aspect of human sex behavior. We are interested in the entire story. The homosexual is a very much larger portion of human sexual behavior than most people realize, and consequently, we have an abundance of data on it, but a proportionately large or larger amount of material on other aspects of human behavior.

¶ From *Dr. Kinsey and the Institute for Sex Research* by Wardell B. Pomeroy (New York: Harper & Row, 1972), p. 139.

The animal research was full of surprises, not the least of which was the revelation of how little was known about the sex lives of even the most familiar animals. We found, for instance, that homosexual activity was as common among animals as it is among humans. One of our field trips took us to the Oregon State Agricultural College farm, where Dr. Fred McKenzie, head of the Department of Animal Husbandry, helped us take about 4,000 feet of moving pictures of sexual behavior in cattle, sheep, hogs and rabbits. Cattle were being bred there for purposes of artificial insemination experiments, and it was not unusual to see cows mounting cows, which we filmed. But our prize came the day Dellenback recorded a bull mounting another bull, achieving complete anal penetration, and ejaculating as he withdrew.

An eminent sex researcher to whom we showed this film remarked: "Every judge in the country who has to deal with sex offenders should see this film.

It might teach him something about what the word 'unnatural' means."

¶ From *Dr. Kinsey and the Institute for Sex Research* by Wardell B. Pomeroy (New York: Harper & Row, 1972), p. 183.

More shocking to many people than the data on premarital and extramarital intercourse were the statistics Kinsey produced on the high incidence and frequency of homosexual behavior in the male population, particularly its coexistence with the heterosexual in the lives of a large part of the male population. In view of these statistics, Kinsey concluded, "it is difficult to maintain the view that psychosexual reactions between individuals of the same sex are rare and therefore abnormal or unnatural, or that they constitute within themselves evidence of neuroses or even psychoses." Needless to say, the controversy these remarks renewed is scarcely settled even now, nearly a quarter century later [1972]. Kinsey believed that homosexual activity would appear in the histories of a much larger portion of the population if it were not for existing social restraints. If it were possible to do what some advocate and eliminate homosexuality from society by isolating and "treating" all those with homosexual tendencies, Kinsey observed, it would mean isolating at least a third of the male population, and if those predominantly homosexual (4 to 6 on the scale he introduced in his book) were to be treated, it would mean isolating at least 13 percent of the male population. Altogether that would mean about 6 1/3 million males. There were many readers — or rather those who read about it in the popular translation — who found themselves profoundly shocked by that figure. Kinsey concluded:

> If all persons with any trace of homosexual history, or those who were predominantly homosexual, were eliminated from the population today, there is no reason for believing that the incidence of the homosexual in the next generation would be materially reduced. The homosexual has been a significant part of human sexual activity ever since the dawn of history, primarily because it is an expression of capacities that are basic in the human animal.

¶ From *Dr. Kinsey and the Institute for Sex Research* by Wardell B. Pomeroy (New York: Harper & Row, 1972), p. 272.

While he was in Copenhagen, Kinsey tracked down a scholar who he knew had amassed an immense pile of data and papers on Hans Christian Andersen [showing that Denmark's literary hero had been a homosexual]. No one in Denmark, Kinsey observed, seemed to know who the scholar was, or that he possessed this comprehensive material. . . . That, Kinsey noted in his journal, was "an excellent illustration of the fact that the world simply must learn that persons with homosexual histories and exclusively homosexual histories have been among the persons who were the most important. I do not share the notion that such persons are the outstanding people, but they certainly have done some of the outstanding things of the world."

¶ From *Dr. Kinsey and the Institute for Sex Research* by Wardell B. Pomeroy (New York: Harper & Row, 1972), p. 409.

A.S. NEILL (1883–1973)

Scottish educator, founder and headmaster of the world-famous Summerhill School.

I wonder how much impotence and frigidity in adults date from the first interference in a heterosexual relationship of early childhood. I wonder how much homosexuality dates from the tolerance of homosexual play and the forbidding of heterosexual play.

Heterosexual play in childhood is the royal road, I believe, to a healthy, balanced adult sex life. When children have no moralistic training in sex, they reach a healthy adolescence — not an adolescence of promiscuity.

¶ From *Summerhill: A Radical Approach to Child Rearing* (New York: Hart, 1960), p. 208.

If we could prevent a child from seeing evil in sex, he would grow up a moral man — not a moralist, not a teacher of others. A Don Juan seemingly fulfills the pleasure component of sex while rejecting the love component. Masturbation, Don Juanism, homosexuality are all unproductive because they are asocial. The new moral man will find that he must fulfill *both* functions of sex: he will find that unless he loves, he will not find the greatest pleasure in the sexual act.

¶ From *Summerhill: A Radical Approach to Child Rearing* (New York: Hart, 1960), p. 222.

There is no homosexuality in Summerhill. However, as in every group of children who come to Summerhill, there is an unconscious homosexuality during a certain stage of development. . . .

Homosexuality is linked in some way to masturbation. You masturbate with the other guy, and he shares the guilt with you, thus lightening your own burden. However, when masturbation is not considered a sin, the necessity to share guilt does not arise.

I do not know what early repressions lead to homosexuality, but it seems quite certain that they must have originated in very early childhood. . . . over a period of thirty-eight years, the school has not turned out a single homosexual. The reason is that freedom breeds healthy children.

¶ From *Summerhill: A Radical Approach to Child Rearing* (New York: Hart, 1960), pp. 234–35.

WALTER WINCHELL (1897–1972)

Gossip columnist and radio personality.

Winchell was a superb editor. A gag man could work hours to condense a topical comment into two lines. Winchell would remove three words and make it punchier. . . .

The Winchell humor leaned quite naturally toward the wisecrack, which was the currency of Broadway. It was topical, brittle, brief and often cruel. He could poke fun at old-world Jews with his Mefoofsky stories and at homosexuals with his jokes about the "pansy" or "limp-wrist" set. He personally enjoyed dirty jokes, and in his early years as a columnist he printed stories that were considered off color by the standards of the time. . . .

¶ From *Winchell* by Bob Thomas (Garden City, N.Y.: Doubleday, 1971), p. 137.

SERGEI EISENSTEIN (1898–1948)

Russian film director (POTEMKIN; ALEXANDER NEVSKY).

In Moscow, even if he could, Eisenstein would not have searched out the perverse in an effort to discover what lay within himself. Reticence would have forbidden it. But in Berlin, where perversity was entirely open to inspection, he attempted to find an answer to his own problem — if there was one. Why could he not love a woman? Why did he dread the sex act? Why was he gripped by the fear that intercourse with a woman would rob him of his creative ability? What made him dread impotence? Freud had given him some speculative answers and led him to sublimation, which now itself might be his secret vice.

Sergei Mikhailovich clothed his search to understand himself in the most impersonally conducted scientific investigation. He went to the *Magnus Hirschfeld Institut fur Geschlechts Wissenschaft*, where every phase of sexual abnormality was being analyzed. There he spent much time studying the phenomena of homosexuality, his reason being the thought that if he had command of knowledge he would detect the signs within himself and control them. In spite of all the great artists who had come into the circle of homosexuality, he felt its practice could lead only to creative death.

Once when discussing this research with me, and his reasons for undertaking it, Sergei Mikhailovich said: "My observations led me to the conclusion that homosexuality is in all ways a retrogression — a going back to the state where procreation came with the dividing of the cells. It's a dead-end. A lot of people say I'm a homosexual. I never have been, and I'd tell you if it were true. I've never felt any such desire, not even towards Grisha, though I think I must in some way have a bi-sexual tendency — like Zola and Balzac — in an intellectual way."

¶ From *Sergei M. Eisenstein* by Marie Seton (New York: Grove, 1960), p. 134.

LORD BEAVERBROOK (SIR WILLIAM MAXWELL AITKEN) (1879–1964)

Canadian-born British newspaper baron.

John Junor of the *Sunday Express* could never understand Beaverbrook's tolerance of homosexuals. Nor could John Gordon, who in his *Sunday Express* column described the Wolfenden report on homosexuality as a "Pansies" Charter. . . . Jean Cocteau and his partner were received without comment at La Capponcina. So was Somerset Maugham, a neighbour. A succession of Beaverbrook's menservants were homosexual or bisexual. He startled one of them, when he was cleaning a bath, by putting his head round the door and rasping, "Are you a homosexual?" Hiring a homosexual for the *Express*, he arranged for him to be given a desk next to a handsome young reporter. He called homosexuals "bugger-boys."

To the end of his life Beaverbrook maintained a keen interest in sexuality — his own and other people's. . . .

¶ From *Beaverbrook: A Life* by Anne Chisholm and Michael Davie (London: Hutchinson, 1992), p. 499.

C.S. LEWIS (1898–1963)

Novelist and essayist (THE SCREWTAPE LETTERS).

[A House Tart was] a pretty and effeminate-looking small boy who acts as a catamite to one or more of his seniors. . . . Though our oligarchy kept most of the amenities of life to themselves, they were, on this point, liberal; they did not impose chastity on the middle-class boy in addition to all his other disabilities. Pederasty among the lower classes [i.e., the younger grades in the school] was not "side," or at least not serious side; not like putting one's hands in one's pockets or wearing one's coat unbuttoned. The gods had a sense of proportion.

The Tarts had an important function to play in making school (what it was advertised to be) a preparation for public life. They were not like slaves, for their favors were (nearly always) solicited, not compelled. Nor were they exactly like prostitutes, for the liaison often had some performance and, far from being merely sensual, was highly sentimentalized. Nor were they paid (in hard cash, I mean) for their services; though of course they had all the flattery, unofficial influence, favor and privileges which mistresses of the great have always enjoyed in adult society. This was where the Preparation for Public Life came in. . . .

One of my friends shared a study with a minor Tart; and except that he was sometimes turned out of the study when one of the Tart's lovers came in (and that, after all, was only natural) he had nothing to complain of. I was not shocked by these things. For me, at that age, the chief drawback to the whole system was that it bored me considerably. For you will have missed the atmosphere of our House unless you picture the whole place from week's end to week's end buzzing, tittering, hinting, whispering about this subject. After games, gallantry was the principal topic of polite conversation; who had "a case with" whom, whose star was in the ascendant, who had whose photo, who had when and how often and what night and where. . . .

I suppose it might be called the Greek Tradition.

¶ From *Surprised by Joy: The Shape of My Early Life* (New York: Harcourt, 1955), pp. 88–89.

There is much hypocrisy on this theme. People commonly talk as if every other evil were more tolerable than this. But why? Because those of us who do not share the vice feel for it a certain nausea, as we do, say, for necrophily? I think that of very little relevance to moral judgment. . . . [H]ow many of those who fulminate on the matter are in fact Christians? And what Christian, in a society so worldly and cruel as that of Wyvery [school] would pick out the carnal sins for special reprobation. Cruelty is surely more evil than lust and the World at least as dangerous as the Flesh. The real reason for all the bother is, in my opinion, neither Christian nor ethical. We attack this vice not because it is the worst but because it is, by adult standards, the most disreputable and unmentionable, and happens also to be a crime in English law. The World will lead you only to Hell; but sodomy may lead you to jail and create a scandal, and lose you your job. . . .

¶ From *Surprised by Joy: The Shape of My Early Life* (New York: Harcourt, 1955), pp. 108–09.

FRANKLIN DELANO ROOSEVELT (1882–1945)

President of the United States, 1933–1945.

Before the Big Three got together, there was a preliminary meeting at the foreign-ministers level in Moscow in late October 1943. The President intended to send Sumner Welles, but the under Secretary of State was forced to resign because of widespread rumors of a homosexual episode with a sleeping-car porter. Roosevelt was saddened by the departure of a longtime friend whose counsel he valued.*

¶ From *FDR: An Intimate History* by Nathan Miller (New York: Doubleday, 1983), p. 494.

COCO CHANEL (1883–1971)

French fashion designer.

Between the start of the war and Coco's return, homosexuality had acquired a kind of official status — if indeed it had not become institutionalized. It was no longer concealed; it was flaunted, particularly in fashion. To Coco this was one more reason for her to join the battle.

"Everyone to his own work," she said. "I spend afternoons in dressing rooms with almost-naked women. Can a man do a job like that? Fiddling with dresses, working with women? I'm naive enough to think it's impossible. Those who do it aren't men." Nevertheless, the male designers who were in the spotlight seemed not at all prepared to yield their eminence to Mademoiselle Chanel. . . .

She said: "Someone came to see me, a gentleman, to ask my advice. He was no longer sure whether he still loved his wife and children or whether he ought to start his life over with a young man. People like that I throw out of the house. They talk to you about their complexes. I'm allergic to

---

* F.D.R. was so angered at William Bullitt, a Welles rival who was said to have spread the rumors about Welles' indiscretions, that he told him he never wanted to see him again. Bullitt got his revenge with a series of postwar articles and books charging that the president's diplomatic blunders had lost the peace.

complexes. All these new words. No one had complexes *before*. They were called vices. I'd rather have people with vices than people with complexes. There've always been people like that, who have to have remarkable complications in order to do the simplest things. Now they're talked about all the time. And that's called sickness now! How can one cure people who don't know whether they love men or women?"

¶ From *Coco Chanel: Her Life, Her Secrets* by Marcel Haedrich, trans. Charles Lam Markmann (Boston: Little, Brown, 1972), pp. 174–75.

From the End of World War II to Today

L. RON HUBBARD (1911–1986)

Founder of Scientology.

The sexual pervert (and by this term dianetics, to be brief, includes any and all forms of deviation in Dynamic II such as homosexuality, lesbianism, sexual sadism, etc., and all down the catalogue of Ellis and Krafft-Ebing) is actually quite ill physically. . . . [T]he pervert is always a very ill person in one way or another, whether he is conscious of it or not. He is very far from culpable for his condition, but he is also so far from normal and so extremely dangerous to society that the tolerance of perversion is as thoroughly bad for society as punishment for it. Lacking proper means prior to this time, society has been caught between tolerance and punishment, and the problem of perversion has, of course, not been resolved. . . .

Hence the pervert, containing hundreds and hundreds of vicious engrams, has had little choice between being dead and being a pervert. But with an effective science to handle the problem, a society which would continue to endure perversion and all its sad and sordid effects doesn't deserve to survive.

¶ From *Dianetics* (New York: Coronet, 1950), pp. 117–18.

MAX LERNER (1902–1992)

American journalist and author.

The fact is that the homosexuals often were a good distance ahead of the armed forces in education and rating and intelligence.

¶ From the *New York Post*, July 20, 1950.

WILLIAM F. BUCKLEY (1925–)

Conservative author, editor, and publisher;
founder of THE NATIONAL REVIEW.

When the civil rights bills were passed in the mid-sixties, their principal sponsor, Senator Hubert Humphrey, promised in one melodramatic session that he would "physically eat" the bill he was promoting if anyone attempted to use his bill in order to prefer a member of one race at the expense of a member of another race. Senator Humphrey died from other causes than the food poisoning to which he'd have been subjected after the Supreme Court OK'd affirmative action.

A fortnight ago we had the Civil Rights Restoration Act, which now extends to the federal government the right to inquire into the racial or sexual composition of a school's basketball team if its medical school is receiving federal subsidies. And last week, Georgetown University, the oldest Jesuit college in America, capitulated on the lawsuit demanding that it make room within Georgetown for gay and lesbian student federations.

One supposes that Georgetown's administrators would at this point interpose that they did not completely lose the fight. True, Georgetown has not been required by the courts to "recognize" the student homosexual groups. But it is required to give the groups facilities. And, it is conceded, the groups will draw their rations from student funds. So far as one can discern, Georgetown's victory is limited to the asterisk it is permitted to use in its catalogue of student activities after Lesbian Liberation Front: "*not officially recognized by the university." To such farthings are the defendants today reduced, if the juggernaut running over them is labelled "civil rights."

In 1952 the Commission on Financing Higher Education of the Association of American Universities issued a warning against the dangers of accepting federal funds. "Under federal control, our hundreds of universities and colleges would follow the order of one central institution, and the freedom of higher education would be lost." Among the signers of that document were the presidents of Harvard, Johns Hopkins, Stanford, and Brown. Those learned gentlemen would take from the situation today whatever satisfaction is desired by profits of doom. But even so, it is hard to imagine that they'd have foreseen a day in which a federal court instructs a religious institution that it is required to countenance, let alone provide quarters for, groups engaged in promoting activity deemed not only wrong but sinful by the moral architects of that institution.

Those who stress (and re-stress) the separation of church and state are certainly narrowing the area within which the freedom of religious exercise is tolerated. Perhaps in the storm cellar. Here is a scenario: A son sues his father for denying him facilities in the home in which to practice homosexuality with a neighbor's son. The ACLU defends the son's freedom on the grounds that the father's house is a beneficiary of a federally backed mortgage, and therefore the civil rights of all its occupants need to be observed.

Lunatic reasoning? Who, ten years ago, would not have thought it lunatic reasoning that a religious institution dedicated to teaching, among other things, the moral law should be obliged to extend its hospitality to those who seek to flout such laws?

I observed with fascination, only a week or so ago, the plausibility with which Senator George McGovern, as ever on the cutting edge of liberal reasoning, defended the recent civil rights extension. It sounds so reasonable to say that "the taxpayers" do not wish their money to be spent on "any institution" that permits the practice of discrimination. Discrimination against race, ethnic background, sex, and now sexual inclination. . . .

Somebody, somewhere, somehow, has got to stop the civil rights thing. It is making a joke out of one after another provision of our Bill of Rights.

¶ From "Terminological Right of Way," in *Happy Days Were Here Again* (New York: Random House, 1993), pp. 48–50.

EDMUND BERGLER (1899–1962)

U.S. psychiatrist, analytic theorist of homosexuality in the 1950s.

I have no bias against homosexuality . . . [but] homosexuals are essentially disagreeable people . . . [exhibiting] a mixture of superciliousness, false aggression, and whimpering . . . subservient when confronted with a stronger person, merciless when in power, unscrupulous about trampling on a weaker person.

¶ From *Homosexuality: Disease or Way of Life* by Edmund Bergler (New York: Hill & Wang, 1956).

Educational mistakes cannot produce homosexuality.

¶ From *One Thousand Homosexuals* (Paterson, N.J.: Pageant Books, 1959).

If information is unavailable, if false statistics are left uncontradicted, if new recruits are not warned by dissemination of the fact that homosexuality is but a disease, the confirmed homosexual is presented with a clear field for his operations — and your teen-age children may be its victims.

¶ From *One Thousand Homosexuals* (Paterson, N.J.: Pageant Books, 1959).

By the end of his life, Bergler became an embarrassment to many serious analysts. His views at conferences and symposia were reported without remark, or they were softened and their offensive edge blunted. Few analytic articles refer to his work. . . .

¶ From *The Psychoanalytic Theory of Male Homosexuality* by Dr. Kenneth Lewes (New York: Simon & Schuster, 1988), p. 153.

NORMAN MAILER (1923–)

*U.S. novelist and essayist (*THE NAKED AND THE DEAD; BARBARY SHORE*).*

. . . I have been as guilty as any contemporary novelist in attributing unpleasant, ridiculous, or sinister connotations to the homosexual (or more accurately, bisexual) characters in my novels. Part of the effectiveness of General Cummings in *The Naked and The Dead* — at least for those people who thought him well-conceived as a character — rested on the homosexuality I was obviously suggesting as the core of much of his motivation. Again, in *Barbary Shore*, the "villain" was a secret police agent named Leroy Hollingsworth whose sadism and slyness were essentially combined with his sexual deviation.

At the time I wrote those novels, I was consciously sincere. I did believe — as so many heterosexuals believe — that there was an intrinsic relation between homosexuality and "evil," and it seemed perfectly natural to me, as well as *symbolically* just, to treat the subject in such a way.

The irony is that I did not know a single homosexual during all those years. I had met homosexuals, of course, I had recognized a few as homosexual, I had "suspected" others, I was to realize years later that one or two close friends were homosexual, but I had never known one in the human sense of knowing, which is to look at your friend's feelings through his eyes and not your own. I did not *know* any homosexual because obviously I did not want to. It was enough for me to recognize someone as homosexual, and I would cease to consider him seriously as a person. He might be intelligent or courageous or kind or witty or virtuous or tortured — no matter. I always saw him as at best ludicrous and at worst — the word again — sinister. (I think it is by the way significant that just as many homosexuals feel forced to throw up protective camouflage, even boasting if necessary of women they have had, not to mention the thousand smaller subtleties, so heterosexuals are often eager to be so deceived for it enables them to continue friendships which otherwise their prejudices and occasionally their fears might force them to terminate.)

Now, of course, I exaggerate to a certain degree. I was never a roaring bigot, I did not go in for homosexual-baiting, at least not face to face, and I never could stomach the relish with which soldiers would describe how they had stomped some faggot in a bar. I had, in short, the equivalent of a "gentleman's anti-Semitism." . . .

Reading [*The Homosexual in America* by Donald Webster Cory] was an important experience. Mr. Cory strikes me as being a modest man, and I think he would be the first to admit that while his book is very good, closely reasoned, quietly argued, it is hardly a great book. Nonetheless, I can think of few books which cut so radically at my prejudices and altered my ideas so profoundly. I resisted it, I argued its points as I read, I was often annoyed, but what I could not overcome was my growing depression that I had been acting as a bigot in this matter, and "bigot" was one word I did not enjoy applying to myself. With that came the realization I had been closing myself off from understanding a very large part of life. This thought is always disturbing to a writer. . . .

So, as I read Mr. Cory's book, I found myself thinking in effect, *My God, homosexuals are people, too.* Undoubtedly, this will seem incredibly naive . . . but prejudice is wed to naivete, and even the sloughing of prejudice, particularly when it is abrupt, partakes of the naive. I have not tried to conceal that note. As I reread this article I find its tone ingenuous, but there is no point in trying to alter it. One does not become sophisticated overnight about a subject one has closed from oneself.

At any rate I began to face up to my homosexual bias. I had been a libertarian socialist for some years, and implicit in all my beliefs had been the idea that society must allow every individual his own road to discovering himself. Libertarian socialism (the first word is as important as the second) implies inevitably that one have respect for the varieties of human experience. Very basic to everything I had thought was that sexual relations, above all else, demand their liberty, even if such liberty should amount to no more than compulsion or necessity. For, in the reverse, history has certainly offered enough examples of the link between sexual repression and political repression. (A fascinating thesis on this subject is *The Sexual Revolution* by Wilhelm Reich.) I suppose I can say that for the first time I understood homosexual persecution to be a political act and a reactionary act, and I was properly ashamed of myself.

. . . At a perhaps embarrassingly personal level, I discovered another benefit. There is probably no sensitive heterosexual alive who is not preoccupied at one time or another with his latent homosexuality, and while I had no conscious homosexual desires, I had wondered more than once if really there were not something suspicious in my intense dislike of homosexuals. How pleasant to discover that once one can accept homosexuals as real friends, the tension is gone with the acceptance. I found that I was no longer concerned with latent homosexuality. It seemed vastly less important, and paradoxically enabled me to realize that I am actually quite heterosexual. Close friendships with homosexuals had become possible without sexual desire or even sexual nuance — at least no more sexual nuance than is present in all human relations.

. . . I have discovered the edges of the rich theme of homosexuality rather than the easy symbolic equation of it to evil. And to that extent I feel richer and more confident as a writer. What I have come to realize is that much of my homosexual prejudice was a servant to my aesthetic needs. In the variety and contradiction of American life, the difficulty of finding a character who can serve as one's protagonist is matched only by the difficulty of finding one's villain, and so long as I was able to preserve my prejudices, my literary villains were at hand. Now, the problem will be more difficult, but I suspect it may be rewarding too, for deep-down I was never very happy nor proud of myself at whipping homosexual straw-boys.

A last remark. If the homosexual is ever to achieve real social equality and acceptance, he too will have to work the hard row of shedding his own prejudices. Driven into defiance, it is natural if regrettable, that many homosexuals go to the direction of assuming that there is something intrinsically superior in homosexuality, and carried far enough it is a viewpoint which is as stultifying, as ridiculous, and as anti-human as the heterosexual's prejudice. Finally, heterosexuals are people, too, and the hope of acceptance, tolerance, and sympathy must rest on this mutual appreciation.

¶ From "The Homosexual Villain," in *Advertisements for Myself* (New York: Signet, 1959), pp. 200–205.

. . . [D.H. Lawrence] had become a man by an act of will, he was bone and blood of the classic family stuff out of which homosexuals are made, he had lifted himself out of his natural destiny which was probably to have the sexual life of a woman, had diverted the virility of his brain down into some indispensable minimum of phallic force — no wonder he worshiped the phallus, he above all men knew what an achievement was its rise from the root, its assertion to stand proud on a delicate base.

¶ From *The Prisoner of Sex* (Boston: Little, Brown, 1971), p. 154.

These are the years [during the writing of *Women in Love*] when he flirts with homosexuality, but is secretly, we may assume, obsessed with it. For he is still in need of that restorative sex he can no longer find, and since his psyche was originally shaped to be homosexual, homosexuality could yet be his peace. Except it could not, not likely, for his mind could hardly give up the lust to dominate. Homosexuality becomes a double irony — he must now seek to dominate men physically more powerful than himself.

¶ From *The Prisoner of Sex* (Boston: Little, Brown, 1971), p. 157.

But homosexuality would have been the abdication of Lawrence as a philosopher-king. Conceive how he must have struggled against it! In all those middle years he moves slowly from the man who is sickened because the other did not yield, to the man who will die because he, himself, will not yield. But he is bitter, and with a rage which could burn half the world. It is burning his lungs.

¶ From *The Prisoner of Sex* (Boston: Little, Brown, 1971), p. 159.

If Lawrence had failed [and given in to homosexuality], how many could find "the pause of peace of our fucking, between us now like a snowdrop of forked white fire"? No, as the male and female blurred into a form which was not yet clearly one, so the center of preoccupation in sex passed from procreation to the "soft, warm, wet" of the polymorphous-perverse, from conception to contraception, from the vagina to the anus, as if the mark of a civilization dying should be a mountainous sense of excitement for the hole which presides over waste. . . . There was homosexuality to survey, all of the castles, drawbridges, penitentiaries, and moats at the back door of every heterosexual urge — the reader might be ready to assume that a look at the work of Jean Genet is near. . . . The real journey would be through homosexuality itself, and since that was a subject some were ready to claim was as large as the hidden half of love, a traveler was obliged to look for a shortcut. What way more direct than to take the inquiry through a jail?

¶ From *The Prisoner of Sex* (Boston: Little Brown, 1971), pp. 161–62.

It is the middle class which looks upon homosexuality as perversion; the upper classes have kept it as a game reserve, and the working classes, to the degree they live in ghettos and are not part of the middle class, take on homosexuality as a species of poor man's copulation — if the money is not present to sheik a bitch for a night, then a smaller man must do. In a slum, the pecking order is equal to the fucking order. In prison, where the social complexities of sexual choice are reduced, and the natural instinct of punishment is to make inmates feel like units, a man can tell to uncomfortably close measure how much he is a man and how much he is a woman by how many ranks of men could lay their dicks on his ass (we are only using the good language of the forces of law and order) as opposed to how many men have asses which are ready to be laid on. It could be said that just as civil society is founded on money, so prison population is founded on the social holdings of prick-on-ass. The most powerful bugger is the mightiest man. Now, this of course is obviously not to say that every convict in every prison finds his place in a chain of buggery — that is true no more than that all men and women in society decide every attitude by money — but it is certainly to say that buggery is as fundamental to prison as money to social life, and so offers a preview of some aspects of the sexual revolution, or does if sex is currency in the single permissive sexual standard. . . . It underlines the fundamental dilemma of homosexuality. If a bugger is a man, if he is indeed twice a man — "a male who fucks a male is a double male," says Darling in *Our Lady of the Flowers* — it is because there is no humiliation more profound in prison than to be at the bottom of the order, to be helpless without a protector, and usable as a female by nearly every other convict. One's ass is one's honor in prison. Men commit murder to defend that ass or to revenge it if it has been raped.

¶ From *The Prisoner of Sex* (Boston: Little Brown, 1971), pp. 164–66.

So, yes, queers in prison strive to become part of the male population, and indeed — it is the irony of homosexuality — try to take on the masculine powers of the man who enters them, even as the studs, if Genet is our accurate guide, become effeminate over the years. For remind us: homosexuality is not heterosexuality. There is no conception possible, no, no inner space, no damnable spongy pool of a womb. Where a man can become more male and a woman more female by coming together in the full rigors of the fuck . . . homosexuals, it can be suggested, tend to pass their qualities over to one another, for there is no womb to mirror and return what is most forceful or attractive in each of them. So the male gets more womanly and the queer absorbs the masculinity of the other — at what peculiar price literature, not science, will be more likely to inform us.

¶ From *The Prisoner of Sex* (Boston: Little Brown, 1971), pp. 171–72.

[Quoted in conversation]:
. . . [T]he main reason for the tremendous popularity of football in America may be our subconscious fascination over the fact that each play starts with the quarterback squatting between the center's legs in the classic pose of sodomy.

JEAN-PAUL SARTRE (1905–1980)

French existentialist philosopher.

Human relations are possible between homosexuals just as between a man and a woman. Homosexuals can love, give, elevate others and elevate themselves. It's surely better to get into bed with a boy friend than to go traveling in Nazi Germany when France has been defeated and strangled.

¶ Quoted in *The Manufacture of Madness* by Dr. Thomas Szasz (New York: Harper & Row, 1970).

The homosexual must remain an object, a flower, an insect, a dweller of ancient Sodom or the planet Uranus, an automaton that hops about in the limelight, anything you like except my fellow man, except my image, except myself. For a choice must be made; if every man is all of man, this black sheep must only be a pebble or must be *me*.

¶ From *Saint Genet, Actor and Martyr* (New York: George Braziller, 1963).

GENE FOWLER (1890–1960)

U.S. journalist, biographer, and novelist.

[In the mid-1930s, there was an influx of homosexuals to Fire Island, where Gene Fowler had made his home. His biographer, H. Allen Smith, asked him how he felt about it.]

[Fowler] frowned. "I'm worried," he said. "I lie in bed at night and worry about them."

"You think they are ruining the island?"

"Oh no, it's not that. The thing that bothers me is: Suppose it turns out that they are right!"

¶ From *The Life and Legend of Gene Fowler* by H. Allen Smith (New York: Morrow, 1977), p. 211.

WILHELM REICH (1897–1957)

Psychoanalyst and sex reformer.

Although Reich has become almost synonymous with "sexual freedom" in some quarters, and his admirers include some gay activists and theoreticians, there is not a single favorable reference to homosexuality in his writings. He loathed homosexuals, never knowingly accepted a homosexual for treatment, and avoided overt homosexuals in his social and professional life. When a Norwegian physician recommended an individual for training with Reich, no sooner had the latter learned of the candidate's homosexuality that he rejected him with the words, "Ich will mit solchen Schweinereien nichts zu tun haben" [I want nothing to do with such filthiness]. In a letter to A.S. Neill in 1948, Reich stated that while his discipline of sex economy dealt with the problems of natural genitality, the sexology promoted by the

World League for Sexual Reform . . . concentrated on lingams, condoms, and homosexual perversions. He had earlier maintained that homosexuality was a disease of fascism that would "wither away" under socialism. Despite all this, the radical wave of the 1960s and later saw counterculture homosexuals turn to Reich as an authority for repudiating conventional morality and equating socialism with the untrammeled gratification of their own sexual impulses.

¶ From *Encyclopedia of Homosexuality*, ed. Wayne R. Dynes (New York: Garland, 1990), pp. 1102–03.

SENATOR JOSEPH R. MCCARTHY (1908–1957)

Anti-communist U.S. senator.

[In the 1950s, McCarthy led the fight against communists and "sex perverts in government." Most of the ninety-one employees dismissed for "moral turpitude" were identified as homosexuals.]

On March 14 [1950] McCarthy himself raised the alleged case of a convicted homosexual who had resigned from the State Department in 1948 but was currently holding a "top-salaried, important position" with the Central Intelligence Agency; he . . . demanded his immediate dismissal: "It seems unusual to me, in that we have so many normal people . . . that we must employ so many very, very unusual men in Washington."

¶ From *Encyclopedia of Homosexuality*, ed. Wayne R. Dynes (New York: Garland, 1990), pp. 786–87.

CHRISTIAN SCIENCE

While we understand homosexuality to be inconsistent with basic Christian teachings, we have deep compassion for all of God's children. Our Church's religious magazines have included testimonies of healing written by individuals who have found freedom from homosexuality.

Jesus' forgiveness of the adulterous woman as recorded in John 8:1–11 sets a Christian standard for us today. Those who were ready to stone her to death were rebuked by Jesus, who then said to the woman, "Neither do I condemn thee: go, and sin no more."

The writings of Mary Baker Eddy, the Discoverer and Founder of Christian Science, are consistent with the foundation Jesus provided. In the chapter entitled "Marriage" in Science and Health with Key to the Scriptures, she describes it as "the legal and moral provision for generation among human kind" (p. 56).

The precepts of Christian Science are based on the teachings and example of Christ Jesus. Jesus taught many important moral lessons, and his Biblical instruction on marriage is always within the context of a relationship between a man and a woman rather than of two people of the same sex.

God, as the Father-Mother of all, creates His children pure and complete. Healing and freedom come with opening one's heart and recognizing this God-given identity, and turning away from mortality.

¶ From *Some Thoughts on Homosexuality* by the Christian Science Committee on Publication (Boston: The First Church of Christ, 1994).

ANTHONY BURGESS (1917–1993)

British author (A CLOCKWORK ORANGE).

There was a time when Americans, ignorant of the as yet uncloseted sodomitic movement in their midst, believed Englishmen to have a monopoly on homosexuality. Ms. Shirley MacLaine, the actress, once called me a "fag" on the strength of my accent. The fact is that many New York homosexuals affect an English accent, probably for purposes of tribal identification as well as distinction from the Lee Marvin-tongued meat-and-potatoes beer-from-a-can men whose notion of sexuality is a Saturday night urge fulfilled in five minutes.

However, there is often a nut of truth in even the most far-fetched fallacy, and it is a fact that adolescent homosexual attachments are acquired in some of the great English public schools, and these very frequently survive into adult life. Indeed, when Britain was run by a public-school-educated governing class, its solidarity was maintained by a sexual culture forgivable only in juveniles.

Still, no one would call homosexuality a specifically English aberration, not now. The best homosexuality is in America, like the best everything else, and California, where all national tendencies achieve their most hyperbolic expression, is a living beach of writhing male bodies.

¶ From "Transatlantic Love Affair," in *Saturday Review*, April 28, 1979, p. 10.

ALAN PATON (1903–1988)

*South African author (*CRY, THE BELOVED COUNTRY; TOO LATE THE PHALAROPE*) and fighter against apartheid.*

It is probable that boys who are abnormally shy of girls enter more easily into homosexual relationships. I entered one such relationship with C., who was in the same class as I but was some two years older. He and I were eating our lunch on the terraces. Just how our conversation proceeded I cannot remember, but it ended up by my feeling his penis, the size and rigidity of which astonished me.

After that I spent the day with him, perhaps two or three times, at his parents' small farm outside the rectangular confines of the city, on which occasions we fondled and masturbated each other. Some two years later, when we were together at the Natal University College, I found a note from him on the notice board. In this letter he expressed his sorrow for what had happened and begged my forgiveness, which I gave freely and briefly by word of mouth.

¶ From *Towards the Mountain* (New York: Scribner, 1980), p. 40.

It is noticeable that Paton did not feel it necessary to ask the friend's forgiveness; neither then nor later was he to give any indication of thinking homosexuality particularly reprehensible, and in old age he was to deny that he had ever condemned it.

¶ From *Alan Paton: A Biography* by Peter F. Alexander (London: Oxford, 1994), p. 29.

When one of [Paton's] staff at Diepkloof [a reformatory] proved to be homosexual, Paton was the one staff member who would have the man in the house.

¶ From *Alan Paton: A Biography* by Peter F. Alexander (London: Oxford, 1994), p. 440 n. 50.

KATHERINE ANNE PORTER (1890–1980)

*American author (*SHIP OF FOOLS; PALE HORSE, PALE RIDER*).*

Although she avoided the parties that had bored her in her first days in Hollywood, she had found a circle of old and new friends.

Among her friends was the fashion photographer George Platt Lynes, whom she had known since her Paris days and whom she had tried to make her lover in spite of her knowledge that he was a homosexual. Although she often spoke contemptuously of homosexuality, she was nevertheless generally tolerant of her homosexual friends, such as Lynes and Glenway Wescott (whose letters to her spoke quite frankly of their affairs with other men, as if they were sure of her sympathetic response), and in the course of her life she was more than once drawn to homosexual men whom she found attractive and desirable as lovers. When they did not return her sexual interest in kind, the humiliation she suffered as a result sometimes turned into vicious invective against homosexuality. Lynes was an exception. In spite of her disappointment that she never managed to have a love affair with him, she remained close friends with him, and when he was put in charge of the Vogue studio in Hollywood, his presence added pleasantly to her social life and contacts.

¶ From *Katherine Anne Porter — A Life* by Joan Givner (New York: Simon & Schuster, 1982), p. 358.

VLADIMIR NABOKOV (1899–1977)

*Russian-American novelist (*LOLITA; PALE FIRE*).*

Nabokov's father was very judgmental about it. The family was sensitive enough about the occurrence of homosexuality, I was told by one Nabokov family member, that Vladimir pere's children were carefully watched for any signs of it, and sexual uncertainty and homosexuality became a major motif in Nabokov's writing.

Homosexuality was always a presence and a problem in the Nabokov family, and that is sufficient explanation for the remarkable gallery of homosexual characters one meets in Nabokov.

When he did talk of *Lolita*, Nabokov would have only two things to say about it: that it was a work of art, and that it had a high moral content. He pointed out with pride that he had received a letter from a man who said that he had abandoned his homosexuality after reading the novel. . . .

¶ From *VN— The Life and Art of Vladimir Nabokov* by Andrew Field (New York: Crown, 1986), pp. 20–21, 39, 306.

SIMONE DE BEAUVOIR (1908–1986)

French novelist and essayist (THE SECOND SEX).

There are also examples of sexually active old age among homosexuals. Should Michelangelo be included? Some people say that his passion for Tommaso Cavalieri was platonic, but the burning sonnets he wrote to him from the day of their first meeting (Michelangelo was fifty-seven) up to his death show feelings unmistakably sexual in origin whether they were sublimated or not. . . . When Gide was over seventy-five he recalled passionate nights of love in his *Journal.* On 3 April 1944, "I cannot bring myself to despise carnal delights, and in any case I make very little effort to do so. An aeroplane breaking down . . . gave me one of the most vivid that can be imagined two nights ago." And on 24 January 1948, "No shame at all after the most casual, easy indulgence that can be imagined."

Proust obviously based his description of Charlus' old age upon flesh-and-blood examples. When young, Charlus gave himself such airs of virility that people who did not know how his tastes lay thought he must be very successful with women. His aristocratic pride stood out against his corruption. His homosexuality appeared only as one of the elements that made up his strong personality. . . .

¶ From *The Coming of Age*, trans. Patrick O'Brien (New York: Putnam, 1972), p. 345.

BILLY GRAHAM (1918–)

American evangelist and religious leader.

Graham showed . . . flexibility in his attitude toward homosexuality and abortion, two . . . issues on which Evangelicals have taken a generally rigid stance. He continued to regard homosexuality as a sin but refused to put it in the category of special heinousness. "The Bible teaches these practices are wrong," he said, "but no more so than adultery." More boldly, he asserted, "I love them and don't treat them any differently than my other friends. There are worse sins." Clearly, he felt that treating homosexuals as pariahs was an un-Christian response. Just as clearly, however, he believed that conversion would lead to a change in sexual orientation, or at least to an ability to control homosexual behavior. "You have to take a vow to God," he recommended, "and ask God to help you, and he will." He recognized that not everyone in his audience would share his views, but rather than write them off as hopeless and hell-bound, he offered them the best advice he could find. In a 1988 telecast focusing on AIDS, he included an extended appearance by Surgeon General C. Everett Koop, who made it clear he believed abstinence was the proper course for unmarried people but urged those who were not being abstinent to use condoms, a notable departure from the standard Evangelical television program.

¶ From *A Prophet with Honor: The Billy Graham Story* by William C. Martin (New York: William Morrow, 1991), p. 585.

KARL BARTH (1886–1968)

Swiss theologian.

[T]he male is a male in the Lord only, but precisely, to the extent that he is with the female, and the female likewise. That they are one in the Lord holds them together. It allows and commands them to be together. And it is the basis of their distinction, which is rooted in the fact wherein they have their essence, namely, that they are directed to be in fellowship. Because their freedom is that which they have from and before and for God, therefore it can take shape only in their fellowship with each other, and their humanity can consist concretely only in the fact that they live in fellow-humanity, male with female, and female with male. Every right of man and woman stands or falls with the observance and maintenance of this rule, and every wrong consists in its contravention.

This rule is from this standpoint the command of God. If we are to be obedient to the divine command we cannot regard ourselves as dispensed from its observance. . . .

. . . [N]either men nor women can seriously wish to be alone, as in clubs and ladies' circles. Who commands or permits them to run away from each other? . . . It is well to pay heed even to the first steps in this direction.

These first steps may well be symptoms of the malady called homosexuality. This is the physical, psychological and social sickness, the phenomenon of perversion, decadence and decay, which can emerge when man refuses to admit the validity of the divine command in the sense in which we are now considering it. In Rom. 1 Paul connected it with idolatry, with changing the truth of God into a lie, with the adoration of the creature instead of the Creator (v. 25). "For this cause God gave them up unto vile affections: for even their women did change the natural use into that which is against nature: and likewise also the men, leaving the natural use of the woman, burned in their lust one toward another; men with men working that which is unseemly, and receiving in themselves the recompense of their error which was meet" (vv. 26–27). From the refusal to recognise God there follows the failure to appreciate man, and thus humanity without the fellow-man. And since humanity as fellow-humanity is to be understood in its root as the togetherness of man and woman, as the root of this inhumanity there follows the ideal of a masculinity free from woman and a femininity free from man. And because nature or the Creator of nature will not be trifled with, because the despised fellow-man is still there, because the natural orientation on him is still in force, there follows the corrupt, emotional and finally physical desire in which — in a sexual union which is not and cannot be genuine — man thinks that he must seek and can find in man, and woman in woman, a substitute for the despised partner. But there is no sense in reminding man of the command of God only when he is face to face with this ultimate consequence, or pointing to the fact of human disobedience only when this malady breaks out openly in these unnatural courses. Naturally the command of God is opposed to these courses. This is almost too obvious to need stating. It is to be hoped that, in awareness of God's command as also of His forgiving grace, the doctor, the pastor trained in psycho-therapy, and the legislator and judge — for the protection of threatened youth — will put forth their best efforts. But the decisive word of Christian ethics must consist in a warning against entering upon the whole way of life which can only end in the tragedy of concrete homosexuality. We know that in its early stages it may have an appearance of particular beauty and spirituality, and even be redolent of sanctity. Often it has not been the worst people who have discovered and to some extent practised it as a sort of wonderful esoteric of personal life. Nor does this malady always manifest itself openly, or, when it does so, in obvious or indictable forms. Fear of ultimate consequences can give as little protection in this case, and condemnation may be as feeble a deterrent, as the thought of painful consequences in the case of fornication. What is needed is that the recognition of the divine command should cut sharply across the attractive beginnings. The real perversion takes place, the original decadence and disintegration begins, where man will not see his partner of the opposite sex and therefore the primal form of fellow-man, refusing to hear his question and to make a responsible answer, but trying to be human in himself as sovereign man or woman, rejoicing in himself in self-satisfaction and self-sufficiency. The command of God is opposed to the wonderful esoteric of this *beata solitudo*. For in this supposed discovery of the genuinely human man and woman give themselves up to the worship of a false god. It is here, therefore, that for himself and then in relation to others each must be brought to fear, recollection and understanding. This is the place for protest, warning and conversion. The command of God shows him irrefutably — in clear contradiction to his own theories — that as a man he can only be genuinely human with woman, or as a woman with man. In proportion as he accepts this insight, homosexuality can have no place in his life, whether in its more refined or cruder forms.

¶ From *Church Dogmatics*, trans. G.W. Bromiley (Edinburgh: T.T. Clark, 1977), vol. 3, bk. 4, pp. 164–66.

GERALDINE FERRARO (1935–)

First woman vice-presidential candidate of a major party in the United States.

My support of gay rights was just as inflammatory to the conservatives. And again, my view was a statement of principle. I believe strongly in equal opportunity for everybody. I don't like discrimination against any group. I'd rather that we all compete on an equal level, without anyone being held back. And I wasn't going to back away from my principles just because my stand might be politically offensive and cost me support. In July I had agreed to speak at a meeting of gay activists in my district. After I got the nomination, the reaction was predictable. "Ms. Ferraro could never be accused of being ambiguous about her support of gays," read a full-page ad "proudly" paid for by the Fund for a Conservative Majority in the Daily News in August. "Last month, she stated . . . 'A victory for a woman in this election is a victory for lesbians and gay men.' "

¶ From *Ferraro: My Story* by Geraldine A. Ferraro with Linda Bird Francke (New York: Bantam, 1985), p. 214.

MARGARET MEAD (1901–1978)

American anthropologist.

As a self-appointed *materfamilias*, she trusted that she knew what was good for people, often better than they might know for themselves. This well-meant help could seem high-handed.

Once Mead went so far as to warn a close friend not to have children, on grounds that she regarded the friend's husband as a latent homosexual, unsuited for fatherhood. "It was meddlesome of Margaret to tell me that," said the friend, who disregarded the advice and so relished being a parent that she only wished, forty years later, that she and her husband had raised several children instead of one, "but I forgave her."

Her long-time psychiatrist acquaintance Rollo May had no doubt she was androgynous. When Mead's Ohio cousin Martha Glardon asked her once what she thought of homosexuals, Mead paused for several seconds and then replied: "They make the best companions in the world." An ideal society,

Mead declared at a 1974 conference, would consist of people who were homosexual in their youth and again in old age, and heterosexual in the middle of their lives. "What is new is not bisexuality," she wrote in one of the last columns on which she and Rhoda Metraux collaborated for *Redbook*, "but rather the widening of our awareness and acceptance of human capacities for sexual love."

Another of Mead's close friends contended that she "fell in love with women's souls and men's bodies. She was spiritually homosexual, psychologically bisexual, and physically heterosexual. She had affairs with both men and women — though never with two men and two women at the same time; in an eccentric way she had a very stern morality — but she wanted people to think there were many more of these affairs than there actually were; 'In our culture,' she said, 'it's good to have the image of the sacred whore.' " . . .

"There's no doubt," said Leo Rosten, "that she spent a great deal of time with groups that included homosexuals, and that those groups found her simpatico, but I don't think that was her own special bent. Pleasure, for her, was an interruption of cerebration. If she had a choice, I always thought, she'd rather exchange ideas than kisses."

¶ From *Margaret Mead: A Life* by Jane Howard (New York: Simon & Schuster, 1984), pp. 15, 367.

LESLIE A. FIEDLER (1917–)

American author and critic.

There is an almost hysterical note to our insistence that the love of male and male does not compete with heterosexual passion but complements it; that it is not homosexuality in any crude meaning of the word, but a passionless passion, simple, utterly satisfying, yet immune to lust — physical only as a handshake is physical, this side of copulation. And yet we can never shake off the nagging awareness that there is at the sentimental center of our novels, where we are accustomed to find their European counterparts "platonic" love or adultery, seduction, rape, or long-drawn-out flirtation, nothing but the love of males! What awaits us are the fugitive slave and the no-account boy side by side on a raft borne by the endless river toward an impossible escape; or the pariah sailor waking in the tattooed arms of the brown harpooner on the verge of some impossible quest. To emphasize the purity of such unions, the fact that they join soul to soul rather than body to body, they are typically contrasted with mere heterosexual passion, the dubious desire which threatens always to end in miscegenation. Yet, though such confrontations seem only to contrast the homoerotic and heterosexual ways of joining white and black, they suggest disconcertingly a general superiority of the love of man for man over the ignoble lust of man for woman.

. . . *Moby Dick* can be read then not only as an account of a whalehunt, but also as a love story, perhaps the greatest love story in our fiction, cast in the peculiar American form of innocent homosexuality.

¶ From *Love and Death in the American Novel* (New York: Stein & Day, 1966), pp. 369–70.

PHYLLIS SCHLAFLY (1924–)

American right-wing crusader against feminist and gay rights.

When Phyllis Schlafly attacked ERA [the Equal Rights Amendment, eventually defeated] on religious grounds, she was, regardless of her arguments' merits, at least being consistent. From the start of her public career, three years after her marriage, it was on religious grounds that she attacked everything from permissive education to bloated bureaucracies. Her arguments that ERA is anti-family and will encourage abortion, homosexuality, and divorce are arguments that one would expect Fred Schlafly [her husband] to mobilize if he were on the front lines fighting ERA.

Schlafly saw several other by-products of ERA over which there was wide disagreement. The amendment's backers denounced these as "scare tactics," arguments that, they said, were about as sound as the flat-earth theory. Schlafly saw ERA as giving homosexuals the right to a marriage license and so the rights of married couples, such as the right to adopt infants. "ERA bans discrimination on account of sex, and it is precisely on account of sex that a state now denies a marriage license to a man and a man." She was not the first person to make this argument. . . .

Saying that Schlafly's style is seldom subtle or understated is, well, an understatement in itself. In Schlafly's lexicon, "pervert" is an acceptable synonym for homosexual. "NOW is for pro-lesbian legislation," Schlafly wrote in her June 1976 *Report*, "so that perverts will be given the same legal rights as husbands and wives such as the right . . . to adopt children and the right to teach school. Surely the right of parents to control the education of their children is a right of a higher order than any alleged right of, say, the two college-educated lesbian members of the Symbionese Liberation Army to teach our young people."

¶ From *The Sweetheart of the Silent Majority: The Biography of Phyllis Schlafly* by Carol Felsenthal (New York: Doubleday, 1981), pp. 111, 238, 273–74.

ABIGAIL VAN BUREN (1918–)

U.S. advice columnist, born
Popo Friedman, Sioux City, Iowa.

Dear Abby:
Our tall, handsome, athletic son served four years in the Navy, returned to civilian life and college, and "married" an undersized, effeminate male hairdresser. We have no idea how to handle this situation or our ambivalent feelings.

This "odd couple" came to visit us, and they want us to visit them. They are inseparable and act out a peculiar husband-wife relationship that is both bewildering and disturbing to us.

So far we have been polite, but what the dickens do you say to friends and relatives? We can't condone it.

We love this boy, but as his parents we feel torn and hypocritical to say the least.
— *Torn*

Dear Torn:
You owe friends and relatives no explanation, so don't feel obligated to offer any. Since your son's lifestyle bewilders and disturbs you, either learn to accept it or quit seeing him.

Dear Abby:
I read with an aching heart the letter in your column from a woman who discovered after ten years and two children that her husband was homosexual. She has my heartfelt sympathy. I have lived in her situation for twenty years, the first ten trying to make it work and the second ten in hell.

If that woman is still young and can support her children, my advice to her would be to get out and never look back.

If she thinks things are bad now, wait until he gets older. Her daily lot will be humiliation, loneliness, and fear of exposure. And she'll never know the luxury of being able to confide in a living soul.

The homosexual is a crippled personality in other ways than sex. This is not textbook talk, I've been there.
— *Twenty-year Stretch*

Dear Stretch:
If, as you say, "a homosexual is a crippled personality," who can blame him? All his life he's heard that he's a "sick, perverted, abominable, loathsome creature," or some kind of freak. He has had to live like a criminal much of the time — for fear someone would "find out" about him. He feels guilty for having "failed" his family. (Is it any wonder the suicide rate for homosexuals is so high?)

I do not know whether homosexuals can be "cured." My medical experts insist that if they are sufficiently motivated, some can. But almost all my mail from homosexuals themselves say that the most they can hope for is "understanding" on the part of others, and the ability to accept themselves as they are and learn to live with it.

Dear Abby:
Recently you printed a letter from someone who claimed to be a "well-adjusted homosexual."

There is no such thing as a well-adjusted homosexual: the two terms are antonymous. Homosexuality, male or female, is a form of sexual deviation which is symptomatic of personality disorder. By any reasonable standard of human development, homosexuality is an abnormal human condition which needs competent professional treatment. It is, in effect, a form of emotional illness.

I think that you would be as interested as I in what your readers think about the subject.
— *Happy Heterosexual*

Dear Happy:
By whose definition is homosexuality an illness? There are homosexuals who live socially well-adjusted, discreet, personally happy lives, whose homosexuality would come as a surprise to many of their close heterosexual friends.

The fact that homosexuality is morally condemned by most people in our culture makes it seem abnormal. In other times and in other cultures it has not always been so judged.

Much of the maladjustment seen in homosexuals is due to the rejection, persecution, and guilt imposed on them by intolerant and ignorant contemporaries.

Dear Abby:
Another advice columnist [Dear Abby's twin sister, Ann Landers!] keeps insisting that homosexuals are "sick." She says, and I quote:

> Thousands of homosexuals have written asking me where they can get 'straightened out,' so they must consider themselves sick — or they wouldn't be asking for help. Occasionally I hear from homosexuals who are at peace with themselves, but they are few and far between.
>
> I believe the majority of homosexuals would be straight if they were really free to choose.

What do you say, Dear Abby?
— *L.A.* Times *Reader*

Dear Reader:
I say if a heterosexual had been raised to believe that his preference for the opposite sex was "sick," twisted, abominable, sinful, and a disgrace to his family, he would ask for help on how to "straighten himself out," too.

Homosexuality is a problem because an unenlightened society has made it a problem, but I have received letters by the thousands (not just "occasionally") from gay people telling me that they wouldn't be straight if they had a choice. All they ask is to be allowed to love in their own way without facing the charge that they are "sick and twisted."

I say, love and let love.

¶ From *The Best of Dear Abby* (Kansas City: Andrews & McMeel, 1981), pp. 64–65, 67–70.

ANN LANDERS (1918–)

Widely syndicated advice columnist, born Eppie Friedman, Sioux City, Iowa.

I believe, when an individual prefers a member of his (or her) own sex as an object of physical love, that person suffers from a severe personality disorder. If a person is — quote — normal — unquote — and if he is given a choice of a person with whom to have sexual contact, he will select a person of the opposite sex.

I was one of the first to fight for homosexual rights. . . . I fought for the civil rights of homosexuals twenty years ago and argued that they should be regarded as full and equal citizens. However, I do not believe homosexuality is "just another life style." I believe these people suffer from a severe personality disorder. Granted some are sicker than others, but sick they are and all the fancy rhetoric of the American Psychiatric Association will not change it.

¶ From *Dear Ann, Dear Abby* by Jan Pottker and Bob Speziale (New York: Dodd Mead, 1987), p. 241.

CUBAN LEGISLATION SINCE THE REVOLUTION

A certain amount of bureaucratization has taken place since the Castro government was formed in 1959, and policy toward homosexuality has been repressive. Criminal legislation provides a fine of three to nine months of imprisonment for the public practice of homosexuality or for soliciting, with heavier penalties when the partner is under 18. In 1965, homosexual faculty at the University of Havana were dismissed, and a number of writers lost their jobs. Three years later, bars in the La Rampa district of Havana were closed, and men suspected of homosexuality on the basis of their style of clothing and haircut were arrested indiscriminately on the streets and inducted into special militarized work units. Homosexuals have been barred from important sectors of the economy: medicine, culture, education, the army, and at least formally, though not always in practice, from party membership. Public statements refer to homosexuality as a form of counter-revolutionary bourgeois depravity and question the loyalty of those who engage in it.

Yet other factors than bureaucracy seem to be at work. The tourist trade under Batista supported male (and female) prostitution, giving it an unsavory reputation. The provisions of the criminal code dealing with homosexuality date back to 1939, cite the Bible, and refer to Sodom, suggesting the continuing influence of Roman Catholicism, rather than a new development.

Cuban contempt for male effeminacy (and to a more limited extent, female masculinity) is also traditional. . . .

[An official statement issued in 1965 declared] No homosexual represents the Revolution, which is a matter for men and not feathers, of courage and not trembling, of certainty and not intrigue, of creative valor and not of sweet surprises.

¶ From *The Construction of Homosexuality* by David F. Greenberg (Chicago: University of Chicago Press, 1988), pp. 441–43.

AMERICAN PSYCHOLOGICAL ASSOCIATION

Homosexuality, per se, implies no impairment in judgment, stability, reliability, or general social or vocational capabilities.

¶ From the Board of Directors, 1975.

AMERICAN PSYCHIATRIC ASSOCIATION

Whereas homosexuality in and of itself implies no impairment in judgment, stability, reliability or vocational capacities, therefore, be it resolved that the American Psychiatric Association deplores all public and private discrimination against homosexuals in such areas as employment, housing, public accommodations, and licensing, and declares that no burden of proof of such judgment, capacity, or reliability shall be placed upon homosexuals greater than that imposed on any other persons.

Further, the APA supports and urges the enactment of civil rights legislation at local, state, and federal levels that would insure homosexual citizens the same protection now guaranteed to others. Further, the APA supports and urges the repeal of all legislation making criminal offenses of sexual acts performed by consenting adults in private.

¶ From a statement issued to the public at the American Psychiatric Association's 1973 annual convention by the Board of Trustees.

ROBERT GORDIS (1908–)

American rabbi, scholar, and author.

This negative attitude toward homosexuality has been maintained by Jewish tradition to the present time. It regards homosexuals as flouting the will of the Creator, who fashioned men and women with different anatomical endowments and with correspondingly distinct roles to play in the sexual process.

All these objections to homosexuality in Judaism were intensified in Christianity because of several additional factors. Most of the converts to the early Christian Church were former pagans who had been exposed to the presence of homosexual practices in their previous environment. Paul, as well as the Church after him, therefore felt it incumbent to attack the practice with all the power at his command. Moreover . . . classical Christianity was basically unhappy with the sexual component of human nature in general. It had to concede that sexual contact was legitimate, first because the instinct cannot be successfully suppressed by most men and women and, second, because it is essential for procreation. Since this last factor is obviously lacking in homosexual activity, there is no justification for yielding to "unnatural lust."

In sum, both Judaism and Christianity, in spite of differences in their approach to sex, have regarded homosexuality as a violation of God's will and a perversion of nature.

. . . We can no longer accept the traditional religious reaction to homosexuality as a horror and an abomination. On the other hand, the fashionable doctrine being propagated in our time — that it is an alternate life style of equal value and legitimacy — must be decisively rejected. Homosexuality is an abnormality, an illness which, like any other, varies in intensity with different individuals. Until more efficacious means are discovered for dealing with their problem, homosexuals deserve the same inalienable rights as do all their fellow human beings — freedom from harassment and discrimination before the law and in society.

There can be no question that homosexuals are entitled to more than justice before the law. It is not enough merely to remove the various kinds of legal disability and overt hostility to which they have long been subjected. Whatever evaluation is placed upon their condition, be it moral, medical, or psychological, they are human beings, our brothers and sisters, who deserve compassion and love from their fellow men and, above all, from their brothers in kinship and in faith.

¶ From *Love and Sex: A Modern Jewish Perspective* (New York: Farrar, Straus, Giroux, 1978), 151, 160–61.

JUSTICE BRYON R. WHITE (1917–)

U.S. Supreme Court Justice on Bowers v. Hardwick case, 1986.

. . . [R]espondent would have us announce, as the Court of Appeals did, a fundamental right to engage in homosexual sodomy. This we are quite unwilling to do. . . .

It is obvious to us that neither of these formulations would extend a fundamental right to homosexuals to engage in acts of consensual sodomy. Proscriptions against that conduct have ancient roots. Sodomy was a criminal offense at common law and was forbidden by the laws of the original 13 states when they ratified the Bill of Rights. In 1868, when the 14th Amendment was ratified, all but 5 of the 37 states in the Union had criminal sodomy laws. In fact, until 1961, all 50 states outlawed sodomy, and today [1986] 24 states and the District of Columbia continue to provide criminal penalties for sodomy performed in private, and between consenting adults. Against the background, to claim that a right to engage in such conduct is "deeply rooted in this nation's history and tradition" or "implicit in the concept of ordered liberty" is, at best, facetious.

CHIEF JUSTICE WARREN BURGER (1907–)

U.S. Supreme Court Justice.

I join the Court's opinion, but I write separately to underscore my view that in constitutional terms there is no such thing as a fundamental right to commit homosexual sodomy.

As the Court notes, the proscriptions against sodomy have very "ancient roots." Decisions of individuals relating to homosexual conduct have been subject to state intervention throughout the history of Western civilization. Condemnation of those practices is firmly rooted in Judeo-Christian standards. . . .

. . . To hold that the act of homosexual sodomy is somehow protected as a fundamental right would be to cast aside millenia of moral teaching.

This is essentially not a question of personal "preferences" but rather of the legislative authority of the state. I find nothing in the Constitution depriving a state of the power to enact the statute challenged here.

JUSTICE LEWIS F. POWELL (1907–)

U.S. Supreme Court Justice.

I join the opinion of the Court.

JUSTICE HARRY A. BLACKMUN (1908–)

U.S. Supreme Court Justice.

This case is [not about] "a fundamental right to engage in homosexual sodomy" as the court proports to declare. . . .

Rather, this case is about "the most comprehensive of rights and the most valued by civilized men," namely "the right to be let alone."

The statute at issue, Georgia Code Ann. Section 16-6-2, denies individuals the right to engage in particular forms of private, consensual sexual activity. . . .

Like Justice Holmes, I believe that "[i]t is revolting to have no better reason for a rule of law than that so it was laid down in the time of Henry IV. It is still more revolting if the grounds upon which it was laid down have vanished long since, and rule simply persists from blind imitation of the past." Holmes, *The Path of the Law* (1897). I believe we must analyze respondent's claim in the light of the values that underlie the constitutional right to privacy. If that right means anything, it means that, before Georgia can prosecute its citizens for making choices about the most intimate aspects of their lives, it must do more than assert that the choice they have made is an "abominable crime not fit to be named among Christians." Herring v. State 119 Ga. 709, (1904). . . .

We protect those rights not because they contribute, in some direct and material way, to the general public welfare, but because they form so central a part of an individual life. We protect the decision whether to marry precisely because marriage "is an association that promotes a way of life, not causes; a harmony in living, not political faiths; a bilateral loyalty, not commercial or social projects" (*Griswold v. Connecticut*). We protect the decision whether to have a child because parenthood alters so dramatically an individual's self-definition, not because of demographic considerations or the Bible's command to be fruitful and multiply. And we protect the family because it contributes so powerfully to the happiness of individuals, not because of a preference for stereotypical households.

Only the most willful blindness could obscure the fact that sexual intimacy is "a sensitive, key relationship of human existence, central to family life, community welfare, and the development of human personality." *Paris Adult Theatre I v. Slayton* (1973). The fact that individuals define themselves in a significant way through their intimate sexual relationships with others suggests, in a nation as diverse as ours, that there may be many "right" ways of conducting those relationships, and that much of the richness of a relationship will come from the freedom an individual has to choose the form and nature of these intensely personal bonds.

In a variety of circumstances we have recognized that a necessary corollary of giving individuals freedom to choose how to conduct their lives is acceptance of the fact that different individuals will make different choices.

For example, in holding that the clearly important state interest in public education should give way to competing claims by the Amish to the effect that extended formal schooling threatened their way of life, the Court declared: "There can be no assumption that today's majority is 'right' and the Amish and others like them are 'wrong.' A way of life that is odd or even erratic but interferes with no rights or interests of others is not to be condemned because it is different." *Wisconsin v. Yoder* (1972). The Court claims that its decision today merely refuses to recognize a fundamental right to engage in homosexual sodomy; what the Court really has refused to recognize is the fundamental interest all individuals have in controlling the nature of their intimate associations with others. . . .

The assertion that "traditional Judeo-Christian values proscribe" the conduct involved, cannot provide an adequate justification for [this anti-sodomy statute of Georgia]. That certain, but by no means all, religious groups condemn the behavior at issue gives the State no license to impose their judgments on the entire citizenry. The legitimacy of secular legislation depends instead on whether the State can advance some justification for its law beyond its conformity to religious doctrine. Thus, far from buttressing his case, petitioner's invocation of Leviticus, Romans, St. Thomas Aquinas, and sodomy's heretical status during the Middle Ages undermines his suggestion that section 16-6-2 represents a legitimate use of secular coercive power. A state can no more punish private behavior because of religious intolerance than it can punish such behavior because of racial animus. . . .

This case involves no real interference with the rights of others, for the mere knowledge that other individuals do not adhere to one's value system cannot be a legally cognizable interest, let alone an interest that can justify invading the houses, hearts, and minds of citizens who choose to live their lives differently.

I can only hope that the Court soon will reconsider its analysis and conclude that depriving individuals of the right to choose for themselves how to conduct their intimate relationships poses a far greater threat to the values most deeply rooted in our nation's history than tolerance of nonconformity could ever do. Because I think the Court today betrays those values, I dissent.

¶ Dissent to *Bowers v. Hardwick* (1986).

PIERRE ELLIOTT TRUDEAU (1919–)

Prime Minister of Canada, 1968–1979, 1980–1984.

The state has no place in the nation's bedroom.

¶ Declared in the federal Liberal cabinet on December 22, 1967, when he was the Minister of Justice.

THE QUAKERS

The Religious Society of Friends, an evangelical Christian religious sect.

"One should no more deplore homosexuality than left-handedness. . . . Homosexual affection can be as selfless as heterosexual affection, and therefore we cannot see that it is in some way morally worse."

¶ From *Toward a Christian View of Sex* by the English Friends, 1963.

We should be aware that there is a great diversity in the relationships that people develop with one another. Although we neither approve nor disapprove of homosexuality, the same standards under the law which we apply to heterosexual activities should also be applied to homosexual activities. As persons who engage in homosexual activities suffer serious discrimination in employment, housing and the right to worship, we believe that civil rights laws should protect them. In particular we advocate the revision of all legislation imposing disabilities and penalties upon homosexual activities.

¶ From the 1973 Philadelphia Yearly Meeting of Friends.

JOHN MONEY (1921–)

Professor of Medical Psychology, Johns Hopkins University.

It is morally wrong to legislate in public the criteria by which the sexual lives of the citizens of Maryland should be conducted intimately and by mutual consent in private. It is also a civic danger to legislate the standards of private, consenting sexual morality with respect, for example, to employability.

Why? Because of the normal variability of erotic practice between consenting adults. Normal variability is so great that the criteria of normalcy for 20% of the population could easily be legislated as the criteria by which to put the remaining 80% in prison. Thus, it is actually possible that a majority of Marylanders could be legislated into prison by reason of copulating with a partner already legally married, or of the wrong legal age, or through the wrong legal orifice, or of the wrong legal sex.

The special issue of HB1004 [the state Bill of Rights] is the issue of sexual orientation with respect to employability in or by the state, which means, in blunt language: Should only self-avowed heterosexuals be employed, or should those who declare themselves bisexual or homosexual also be employed? . . .

Statistically, the most conservative estimate, based on self-disclosure, is that 3% of the population is, in terms of erotic partner, exclusively homosexual. That means, in the population of Maryland, that 120,000 people would be unemployable, during the working years of their lives, if legislatively discriminated against because of their sexual orientation. The actual figure could be as high as 200,000, with men more frequently represented than women. These figures are for people who are not heterosexual during any period of their lives.

Primarily heterosexual people who have an admitted homosexual experience at some point in their lives after puberty constitute an estimated one-third of the population, at least. That means that an estimated 1,300,000 people would become unemployable if Maryland law made it necessary to discriminate against them sexually. That is to say, 2 out of every 3 people in the state might, sooner or later, become obliged to support the 3rd, should he/she be legislated into jail or onto welfare because of sexual unemployability, despite his/her capacity to work. Many of these "sexual unemployables" would be at the highest level of education, politics, government, business, industry, and the professions, for homosexuality, heterosexuality, and bisexuality are found at all levels of society.

Medical science has not yet found the formula to explain, predict, or control a person's sexual orientation, whether it be homosexual, bisexual, or heterosexual. . . .

There is an analogy also with handedness. Some people are left-handed, some ambidextrous, and some right-handed. The cause is not fully explainable, though there does appear to be an innate plus a learned component.

The same applies to homosexuality, bisexuality, and heterosexuality. It used to be fashionable for schoolteachers to punish left-handed children in an effort to make them right-handed. Today it is still fashionable to punish the homosexual (and bisexual) people, as in job discrimination. The punishment is ineffectual, for it is not possible to force a change from homosexuality to bisexuality, any more than it is possible to force a heterosexual person into becoming a homosexual.

Homosexual and bisexual people are not a danger to society any more than are heterosexuals. The vast majority lead useful, productive lives, practicing their personal sexual preference as privately as heterosexuals do theirs. The protection of their privacy should be legal. The nobility of the law requires it.

¶ From "Statement on Antidiscrimination Regarding Sexual Orientation," in *Journal of Homosexuality* 2, no. 2 (Winter 1976–77), pp. 159–61.

The folkways of our culture are filled with images of homosexuals as sick, evil, less than human. There are so many signals from the home, the school, the church — and from the media, which makes homosexuality the daily butt of television humor and have given such publicity to Anita Bryant and her gays-are-child-molesters campaign as to legitimate her views, especially in the eyes of our youth. At the same time, the law itself epitomizes this attitude. The very fact that our laws make homosexuality a crime puts the stamp of approval on the idea that "queers" are animals.

Look, it's like a farm kid who proves his manhood by going out and shooting a deer. There are no wild animals in our cities, but the society's values make the homosexual a "faggot," easy prey, an urban animal.

¶ Interview in September 1979, about the uproar over the struggle for a gay-rights bill in Florida.

NORMAN PODHORETZ (1930–)

American editor of COMMENTARY *magazine, author (*MAKING IT*), and leading neo-conservative thinker.*

. . . I *had* chosen a life of middle-class respectability in many essential respects. I was married and I believed in marriage; I had children and I believed in having them. I had a steady job and I believed in working hard. The notion that all this represented a form of suicide — spiritual, emotional, and sexual suicide — I knew to be simply ridiculous in my case, and I had no reason to think that it was any the less ridiculous in the case of others.

Most of the time I didn't feel defensive at all about these matters. Far from it. In that period of my life there was nothing that appealed to me less than the idea of refusing to grow up and settle down — which, stripped of all the rhetoric and all the ideology, was what Kerouac and Ginsberg and their friends stood for — and nothing that I wanted more than to take my rightful place as an adult among other adults. They feared maturity and the responsibilities it entailed as a limitation of their freedom. In fact, one of the reasons so many of them were tempted into homosexuality was that it allowed them to avoid becoming husbands and especially fathers — it was a way of never growing up, of trying to remain forever young. My ambitions ran in exactly the opposite direction. As a child I couldn't wait to grow up; as a young man I was eager to get married, and so far from unwilling was I to become a father that when I did get married it was to a woman who already had two little children for me to raise while waiting for my own to be born.

¶ From *Breaking Ranks* (New York: Harper & Row, 1979), p. 28.

ERICH FROMM (1900–1980)

German-born psychoanalyst and philsopher, author of *ESCAPE FROM FREEDOM; THE SANE SOCIETY.*

Thus far I have spoken of love as the overcoming of human separateness, as the fulfillment of the longing for union. But above the universal, existential need for union rises a more specific, biological one: the desire for union between the masculine and feminine poles. The idea of this polarization is most strikingly expressed in the myth that originally man and woman were one, that they were cut in half, and from then on each male has been seeking for the lost female part of himself in order to unite again with her. (The same idea of the original unity of the sexes is also contained in the Biblical story of Eve being made from Adam's rib, even though in this story, in the spirit of patriarchalism, woman is considered secondary to man.) The meaning of the myth is clear enough. Sexual polarization leads man to seek union in a specific way, that of union with the other sex. The polarity between the male and female principles exists also *within* each man and each woman. Just as physiologically man and woman each have hormones of the opposite sex, they are bisexual also in the psychological sense. They carry in themselves the principle of receiving and of penetrating, of matter and of spirit. Man — and woman — finds union within himself only in the union of his female and his male polarity. This polarity is the basis for all creativity.

The male-female polarity is also the basis for interpersonal creativity. This is obvious biologically in the fact that the union of sperm and ovum is the basis of the birth of a child. But in the purely psychic realm it is not different; in the love between man and woman, each of them is reborn. (The homosexual deviation is a failure to attain this polarized union, and thus the homosexual suffers from the pain of never-resolved separateness, a failure, however, which he shares with the average heterosexual who cannot love.)

The same polarity of the male and female principle exists in nature; not only, as is obvious in animals and plants, but in the polarity of the two fundamental functions, that of receiving and that of penetrating. It is the polarity of the earth and rain, of the river and the ocean, of night and day, of darkness and light, of matter and spirit.

¶ From *The Art of Loving* (New York: Bantam, 1963), pp. 27–28.

LORD ARRAN (1910–1983)

British Liberal peer, journalist, and supporter of the Homosexual Law Reform Society in the 1960s; member of the House of Lords.

[The Sexual Offences Act passed through the House of Commons, received Royal Assent on July 27, 1967, and immediately became law throughout England and Wales. The old law of Henry VIII remains in both Scotland and Northern Ireland. The new act legalized homosexual acts between consenting adults in private.]

[I speak] as an ordinary man, who is privileged to be a Member of your Lordships' House, and as a Christian. . . .

I have read much on this subject, so much, indeed, that at times the issues became blurred, and I no longer knew what it was all about. But, in the end, having read all, or most, of the books, and absorbed to the best of my ability all the clever arguments and counter-arguments, I found myself back where I started, and with these conclusions: that, in accepting the law on homosexual practices as it now stands, we are persecuting a minority and we are being unjust. And these things, I think, are unbecoming to our country.

¶ From a speech before the House of Lords, May 12, 1965, quoted in *The Other Love: An Historical and Contemporary Survey of Homosexuality in Britain* by H. Montgomery Hyde (London: Heinemann, 1970).

I know that there are dangers in this Bill. There are dangers in all reform. I suppose there was a danger in the Bills for the abolition of hanging for sheep stealing and for slavery. These things seemed to a number of wise people at the time to be wrong; but they were done, and Britain survived and was the better for it.

¶ From a speech introducing the Bill for its successful Second Reading on May 10, 1966, quoted in *The Other Love: An Historical and Contemporary Survey of Homosexuality in Britain* by H. Montgomery Hyde (London: Heinemann, 1970).

When we first debated these affairs — and how long ago it seems! — I said that your Lordships had it in your power to remove fear from the hearts of men. This you have done. It was this House that gave the lead. Because of the Bill now to be enacted, perhaps a million human beings will be able to live in greater peace. I find this an awesome and marvellous thing. . . . My Lords, Mr. Wilde was right: the road has been long and the martyrdoms many, monstrous and bloody. Today, please God! sees the end of that road.

Lest the opponents of the Bill think that a new freedom, a new privileged class, has been created, let me remind them that no amount of legislation will prevent homosexuals from being the subject of dislike and derision or at best of pity. We shall always, I fear, resent the odd man out. That is their burden for all time, and they must shoulder it like men — for men they are.

¶ Quoted in *The Other Love: An Historical and Contemporary Survey of Homosexuality in Britain* by H. Montgomery Hyde (London: Heinemann, 1970), p. 268.

U.S. BLACK LIBERATION MOVEMENT

Revolutionary nationalists and genuine communists cannot uphold homosexuality in the leadership of the Black Liberation Movement. . . .

Homosexuality is a genocidal practice. . . .

Homosexuality does not birth new warriors for liberation. . . . [It] is an accelerating threat to our survival as a people and as a nation.

¶ From a leaflet distributed at American meetings of black nationalists, 1981.

UNITARIAN UNIVERSALIST ASSOCIATION OF CHURCHES IN NORTH AMERICA

Discrimination Against Homosexuals and Bisexuals: Recognizing that

1. A significant minority in this country are either homosexual or bisexual in their feelings and/or behavior;
2. Homosexuality has been the target of severe discrimination by society and in particular by the police and other arms of government;
3. A growing number of authorities on the subject now see homosexuality as an inevitable sociological phenomenon and not as a mental illness;
4. There are Unitarian Universalists, clergy and laity, who are homosexuals and bisexuals;

THEREFORE BE IT RESOLVED: That the 1970 General Assembly of the Unitarian Universalist Association: 1) Urges all people immediately to bring an end to all discrimination against homosexuals, homosexuality, bisexuals, and bisexuality, with specific immediate attention to the following issues:

Private consensual behavior between persons over the age of consent shall be the business only of those persons and not subject to legal regulations. Urges all churches and fellowships, in keeping with our changing social patterns, to initiate meaningful programs of sex education aimed at providing a more open and healthier understanding of sexuality in all parts of the United States and Canada, and with the particular aim to end all discrimination against homosexuals and bisexuals.

¶ General Assembly, 1970.

SOUTHERN BAPTISTS

U.S. religious movement.

Whereas, homosexuality has become an open lifestyle for increasing numbers of persons, and

Whereas, attention has focused on the religious and moral dimensions of homosexuality, and

Whereas, it is the task of the Christian community to bring all moral questions and issues into the light of biblical truth;

Now therefore, be it resolved that the members of the Southern Baptist Convention . . . affirm our commitment to the biblical truth regarding the practice of homosexuality and sin.

Be it further resolved, that this Convention, while acknowledging the autonomy of the local church to ordain ministers, urges churches and agencies not to afford the practice of homosexuality any degree of approval through ordination, employment, or other designations of normal lifestyle.

Be it further resolved, that we affirm our Christian concern for all persons saved from the penalty and power of sin through our Lord Jesus Christ, whatever their present individual lifestyle.

¶ From *Resolution on Homosexuality*, 1976.

THE GREEK ORTHODOX CHURCH

The Orthodox Church condemns unreservedly all expressions of personal sexual experience which prove contrary to the definite and unalterable function ascribed to sex by God's ordinance and expressed in man's experience as a law of nature.

Thus the function of the sexual organs of a man and a woman and their biochemical generating forces in glands and glandular secretions are ordained by nature to serve one particular purpose, the procreation of the human kind.

Therefore, any and all uses of the human sex organs for purposes other than those ordained by creation, runs contrary to the nature of things as decreed by God. . . .

The Orthodox Church believes that homosexuality should be treated by society as an immoral and dangerous perversion and by religion as a sinful failure. In both cases, correction is called for. Homosexuals should be accorded the confidential medical and psychiatric facilities by which they can be helped to restore themselves to a self-respecting sexual identity that belongs to them by God's ordinance.

¶ From Biennial Clergy-Laity Congress, 1976.

MASTERS AND JOHNSON

William Masters (1915–) and Virginia Johnson (1925–), sex researchers and authors (HOMOSEXUALITY IN PERSPECTIVE).

What we have tried to do in *Homosexuality in Perspective* is to call upon the resources we developed to treat heterosexual dysfunction and apply them to homosexuals, something that really has not been done before. We can now state with real security that there simply is no difference between the facility (capacity or efficiency) of heterosexuals and homosexuals to respond to sexual stimulation. Nor is there any difference between males and females, homosexual or heterosexual, for such capacity.

We happen to think that heterosexuality is also a learned behavior. We do not believe that we are born homosexual or heterosexual, but male and female sexual entities.

We have no concept of homosexuality as maladaptive. That is a value judgment we do not make or feel, or find present in our work.

We found that the dysfunctional subjects were interested in functioning effectively as homosexuals, *not* as heterosexuals.

¶ From an interview with Lawrence Mass in *Dialogues of the Sexual Revolution* (New York: Harrington Park Press, 1990), pp. 3, 4, 6.

DR. MARY CALDERONE (1914–)

Sex educator, founder of the Sex Information and Education Council of the United States (SIECUS), and author (THE FAMILY BOOK ABOUT SEXUALITY).

The truth is that when I made [homophobic] statements the literature on homosexuality was scarce and printed opinion was still extremely conservative and distorted. Many of the important developments in the understanding of homosexuality had not yet taken place. On the other hand, when I began in this field in 1964, I certainly had to be a victim of some of the prejudices of my time and place. The interesting thing is that such prejudice is so pervasive that it tends to operate unconsciously. I had never actually thought of myself as homophobic. Well, I had a lot to learn. It wasn't until I became involved with SIECUS that I was able to update my understanding of sexual variance. In fact, I wrote to the *Journal of the American Medical Association* urging substitution of *variant* for *deviant*, because the latter was pejorative. A major influence in the evolution of my thinking was my first gay film. Here, a real-life couple was shown making *love*. From that time on, I had no more doubts that homosexuals are doing and feeling exactly the same things that heterosexuals — and I myself — enjoy.

To arrive at my present thinking and statements about homosexuality, I had to do a lot of growing, and that's exciting. Even at my great age of 76, I am continually learning, changing and my life is immeasurably enriched by the privilege of growth. As you know, my present position on homosexuality is not just supportive, it's outspokenly realistic. The reason is that I deeply believe it's the heterosexuals, those who are in power, who should be standing up for gay rights. Unfortunately, gay people are having to fight battles practically alone, in much the same way that blacks, women, and too many other minorities in America have had to struggle for their fundamental human freedoms. Ha! In coming out so strongly for the rights of gay people, I suppose [I run] the "risk" of being labeled homosexual myself. . . .

¶ From an interview with Lawrence Mass in *Dialogues of the Sexual Revolution* (New York: Harrington Park Press, 1990), pp. 66–67.

THE SIECUS/NYU PRINCIPLES BASIC TO EDUCATION FOR SEXUALITY, 1980

— The expression of sexual orientation is a fundamental human right.
— The majority of individuals have some elements of both homosexuality and heterosexuality in their makeup which may or may not be identified or expressed by the individual throughout his or her life.
— Social structures or attitudes which lead to repression of sexuality in general, and homosexuality and bisexuality specifically, may cause individual and interpersonal difficulties.
— The sexual orientation of any person, whether child, adolescent, or adult, cannot be changed solely by exposure to other orientations. Occasional experiences are not necessarily indicative of a person's sexual orientation.
— It is the right of every individual to live in an environment of freely available information, knowledge and wisdom about sexuality, so as to be enabled to realize his or her human potential.

¶ Quoted in *Dialogues of the Sexual Revolution* by Lawrence Mass (New York: Harrington Park Press, 1990), pp. 69–70.

DR. THOMAS SZASZ (1920–)

*American psychoanalyst and author (*LAW, LIBERTY AND PSYCHIATRY; THE MYTH OF MENTAL ILLNESS*).*

If moral values are to be discussed and promoted, they ought to be considered for what they are — moral values, not health values.

We delude ourselves . . . if because of its biological value, we accept heterosexuality as a social value. The jump from biological value to social value is the crux of human morality.

. . . My contention that the psychiatric perspective on homosexuality is but a thinly disguised replica of the religious perspective which it displaced, and that its efforts to treat this kind of conduct medically are but thinly disguised methods of repressing it, may be verified by examining any contemporary psychiatric account of homosexuality.

> . . . [P]sychiatric pre-occupation with the disease concept of homosexuality . . . conceals the fact that homosexuals are a group of medically stigmatized and socially persecuted individuals.

Ever since the Freudian revolution, and especially since the Second World War, it has become intellectually fashionable to hold that homosexuality is neither a sin nor a crime but a disease. This claim means either that homosexuality is a condition somewhat similar to ordinary organic maladies, perhaps caused by some genetic error or endocrine imbalance, or that it is an expression of psychosexual immaturity, probably caused by certain kinds of personal and social circumstance in early life.

I believe it is very likely that homosexuality is, indeed, a disease in the second sense and perhaps sometimes even in the stricter sense. Nevertheless, if we believe that, by categorizing homosexuality as a disease, we have succeeded in removing it from the realm of moral judgment, we are in error.

¶ From "Legal and Moral Aspects of Homosexuality," in *Sexual Inversion: The Multiple Roots of Homosexuality*, ed. Judd Marmor (New York: Basic Books, 1965), p. 124.

MARSHALL MCLUHAN (1911–1980)

Canadian media interpreter, professor, and author (UNDERSTANDING MEDIA; THE GUTENBERG GALAXY).

According to McLuhan, the Cambridge of his day was also full of homosexuals. This was another exaggeration, although Cambridge homosexuals, like the Communists (and the two were often the same), wielded an influence out of proportion to their numbers. Homosexuality at Cambridge tended to express itself in a sort of hyperaestheticism, which McLuhan found almost as distasteful as Marxism. If social life often boiled down to a war between the "hearties" and the aesthetes, McLuhan, with his rowing oar, ultimately preferred the hearties. (When he had tea with fellow Trinity Hall student Robin Maugham, for example, he was appalled by Maugham's arty friends.) Certainly from Cambridge onward, he had an absolute disregard for aesthetes and removed himself from any temptation to play the role of lover of beauty. He was never interested, for example, in the "music of words" in poetry, and his tastes in painting and music were doubtful at best.

¶ From *Marshall McLuhan: The Medium and the Messenger* by Philip Marchand (New York: Random House, 1989), pp. 39–40.

In McLuhan's eyes, Dagwood [the cartoon character, ever childlike and ineffectual], the mama's boy and the homosexual were closely related figures. Grand sociological theories aside, he had been horrified by the "homosexual cult" since his Cambridge years and retained throughout his life the repugnance of a strait-laced Methodist child for homosexual activity. During his later years he was very careful to keep his opinion to himself, but throughout the 1940s his distaste was transmuted into a significant, if discreet, motif of his social criticism. He feared that male homosexuality was rampant in the age, the result of Blondie's emasculating Dagwood in front of Cookie and Alexander, their children. Such homosexuality was probably the chief threat to contemporary morality.

¶ From *Marshall McLuhan: The Medium and the Messenger* by Philip Marchand (New York: Random House, 1989), p. 66.

SUSAN BROWNMILLER (1935–)

U.S. feminist and author (FEMININITY).

Within the current Gay Liberation Movement there is a boisterous minority contained within the outposts of leather bars that would like to see consensual sadomasochism, including the paraphernalia of whips and handcuffs, accepted as a civil-libertarian right, as drag queens are demanding the right to dress in traditionally female attire. Again, what is a feminist to make of this? Does homosexual sadomasochism have its own, peculiarly male, dynamic, or is it an aberration masquerading as the newest issue? The international language of sadomasochism, from the prison argot to the intellectual's musing, and its immutable rites and practices are too revealing to ignore. Sartre explains for Genet that "the rump is the secret femininity of males, their passivity," and both men agree that passivity is defined as being on the receiving end of a penis. In the man-on-man definition, fellatio, too, is a passive act and cocksucker is the equivalent of chicken. Hardly by accident, sadomasochism has always been defined by male and female terms. It has been codified by those who see in sadism a twisted understanding of their manhood, and it has been accepted by those who see in masochism the abuse and pain that is synonymous with Woman. For this reason alone sadomasochism shall always remain a reactionary antithesis to women's liberation.

Although I believe that masochism is often a dynamic in homosexuality, I am not suggesting that it is in some way integral to noncoercive, one-sex relationships or predilections. More significant, perhaps, than the masochistic factor has been the blanket assumption of masochism — in the belief that all male homosexuals wish to be forcibly violated — that has been used with telling effect by heterosexual men who wish to avoid the implications and reality of a man's rape by other men. Here again, the parallels to the woman's experience are obvious. I have listened more than once to the story of a homosexual youth who tried without success to convince his local precinct that he was beaten and raped by some strangers he met in a gay bar and thoughtlessly decided to entertain at home. To the cops in the precinct, the raped youth was nothing more than a faggot who was "asking for it." Along the same lines, T.E. Lawrence's account of his gang rape by the soldiers of the Nuri Bey in Deraa, laundered in many editions of Seven Pillars of Wisdom, has been quartered and dissected by a host of Lawrence scholars who feel that the "truth" of the brutal sodomizing hangs on Lawrence's alleged or suppressed homosexuality. Indeed, I have heard the argument that Lawrence's sphincter muscles should have been sufficient to ward off unwelcome penetration. Correspondingly, some modern sociologists have tried to downplay homosexual rape in American prisons by making use of the biased belief that — this is a direct quote from an accepted source — "there is some question, as in heterosexual situations, as to whether the situation is really in fact rape or whether it is a seduction which has simply gone wrong."

¶ From *Against Our Will: Men, Women and Rape* (New York: Simon & Schuster, 1975), pp. 263–64.

ROBERT BLY (1926–)

U.S. poet and men's movement guru, author of IRON JOHN.

In the seventies I began to see all over the country a phenomenon that we might call the "soft male." Sometimes even today when I look out at an audience, perhaps half the young males are what I'd call soft. They're lovely, valuable people — I like them — they're not interested in harming the earth or starting wars. . . .

But many of these men are not happy. You quickly notice the lack of energy in them. They are life-preserving but not exactly life-giving. Ironically, you often see these men with strong women who positively radiate energy.

¶ From *Iron John: A Book about Men* (New York: Addison-Wesley, 1990), pp. 2–3.

SYDNEY J. HARRIS (1917–)

Popular U.S. journalist and columnist.

The public examination of homosexuality in our contemporary life is still so coated with distasteful moral connotations that even a reviewer is bound to wonder uneasily why *he* was selected to evaluate a book on the subject, and to assert defensively at the outset that he is happily married, the father of four children, and the one-time adornment of his college boxing, track, and tennis teams.

¶ From "The Hidden Crowd," a review of *The Sixth Man* by Jess Stearn, in *Saturday Review*, April 22, 1961, p. 27.

LILLIAN HELLMAN (1905–1984)

U.S. playwright and author
*(*THE CHILDREN'S HOUR; THE LITTLE FOXES*).*

I still have a diary entry . . . asking myself whether talk about the size of the male organ isn't a homosexual preoccupation: if things aren't too bad in other ways I doubt if any woman cares very much.

¶ From *Pentimento: A Book of Portraits* (Boston: Little, Brown, 1973).

ELIZABETH L. POST (1920–)

U.S. expert on etiquette (a.k.a. Emily Post).

Just as stereotyped roles in marriage have been rejected, so have stereotyped images of men and women in hundreds of minority groups in the world around us. Not yet "have been rejected," perhaps, but "are being rejected" with legal help and human understanding. The disabled have been invited into the mainstream of life. Homosexuals are allowed to emerge from the closet. Mixed marriages are taking place every day. We have come a long way in recognizing that people are individually created, not stamped from a mold in the shape of a majority group.

¶ From *Emily Post's Etiquette*, 14th ed. (New York: Harper & Row, 1984), p. 146.

DESMOND MORRIS (1928–)

British zoologist and author (THE NAKED APE; THE HUMAN ZOO; BODYWATCHING).

For the vast majority of humans, then, sexuality takes the form of heterosexual pairing and the establishment of a breeding family unit, accompanied by a certain amount of extra-family sexual activity. In our mainstream cultures, approximately ninety per cent of the population will follow this pairing pattern and about half of those will eventually, at some point, participate in extra-pair copulations.

There is, however, quite a large minority today that steps outside this ancient pattern and establishes a different lifestyle which denies the reproductive cycle. These non-breeders are most common in large, urban communities where the population density has soared to startling new heights.

Celibates, bachelors, spinsters, eunuchs, monks, nuns and homosexuals are all valuable non-contributors to the population explosion that threatens to destroy our species. Because they leave no children behind them, their blood-line stops with them and their genetic influence on their species vanishes as soon as they die.

It is no accident that, as human overcrowding has worsened year by year, homosexual behaviour has become increasingly tolerated by heterosexuals. Earlier attitudes, which saw homosexuality as "sinful" and "perverted," and made it unlawful, are now changing. For many people, hatred has been replaced by sympathy. In the popular mind, homosexuals may still not be fully accepted but they have at least graduated from being "wicked" to being somehow "sexually disabled." This has dramatically reduced the levels of persecution that they have had to endure in the past.

In any other animal a non-breeding adult would have to be counted as a biological failure, contributing nothing to the history of their species, but with humans this is not the case. With us, there is always the possibility of a lasting, non-genetic influence of some kind. Many non-breeding individuals pass on a cultural legacy, through their works of art, their scientific discoveries and other such achievements. So all is not lost, even if they have stepped outside the genetic sequence.

There have been many arguments concerning the cause of homosexuality. If, as described earlier, there is a complex set of gender signals to which we are attuned as a species, then how can this crucial breeding system misfire so dramatically? How can our primeval urge to reproduce be misdirected so easily?

It has been suggested that there is a "homosexual gene" and that homosexuality is a pattern of behaviour with which certain individuals are born. The folly of this argument is that any gene that reduces reproductive success will, inevitably, destroy itself. It is much more reasonable to suppose that there is something in the personal histories of homosexuals that accounts for their sexual preferences.

It is important to realize that there are two different aspects to homosexual behaviour. First, there is the use of a member of the same gender as a partner simply because of the absence of the opposite sex. Sailors at sea for long periods, criminals confined to prison and schoolchildren in unisex boarding schools may all engage in homosexual acts on the basis that they are "better than nothing." When returned to the ordinary, social world, they quickly revert to heterosexual activities.

Quite distinct from such individuals are those who actively prefer the same sex, even when the opposite sex is readily available. In extreme cases they are quite incapable of interacting sexually with the opposite sex, even when attempting to do so. They have no choice but to form same-sex pair-bonds and establish themselves as pseudo-family units, often adopting animals as substitute children, as a way of satisfying their unfulfilled and unfulfillable parental urges.

Such individuals have usually experienced some kind of sexual malimprinting during childhood. When we first experience sexual sensations at the start of puberty, one of two things happens to us. We either gain our sexual awareness in a vague, gradual way, little by little, or it arrives as an intense, memorable moment. If there is a particular something or someone present during a sharp, intense, awakening, then we have a tendency to become imprinted on that special feature. We endow it, or them, with a powerful sexual significance. If, as so often happens, we are sexually inhibited and shy at this early stage, then the special feature of our first, unforgettable experience looms larger and larger in our imaginations until we become fixated on it.

This is the background of many of our sexual oddities. All fetishists seem to begin their sexual histories in this way. If their initial arousals happened to be associated with objects made of leather, rubber or fur, then such substances may take on a super-sexual significance in later life. If the crucial element happened to be a member of the same sex, then that too would bias the subsequent, adult activities. . . .

Why do the genes bother with us? Because, for them, we are a convenient way of maintaining some degree of flexibility. By juggling them around, courtesy of copulation, we keep their options open. We give them the chance of slight changes that will help them to survive a little better in an ever shifting world. Without us, they would become too fixed, too rigid, and could easily perish.

For them, the worst catastrophe is for us to fail to reproduce. If we do that, we are genetic disasters. The gene stops there. For every celibate — every bachelor, spinster, monk, nun and full-time homosexual, the failure to breed means that the millions of years of evolution that led to the ultimate formation of their sperm and eggs have come to a juddering halt. Their line is ended. Their potential immortality is no more.

For the rest of us, our children give us our genetic immortality. Our parents have handed on to us the chromosomal baton in the relay race of life and we have taken up the challenge by becoming parents ourselves. Ensuring that our genes continue without mishap in the new containers we have provided for them, we suddenly find ourselves overwhelmed by a desire to become loving, caring parents.

¶ From *The Human Animal: A Personal View of the Human Species* (London: BBC Publications, 1994), pp. 148, 150–51, 156.

FIELD MARSHAL BERNARD MONTGOMERY (1887–1976)

British war hero.

To the press, David announced his father had "mellowed. . . . Having spent most of his life making his views felt, he now feels he has done his bit and is very peaceful and philosophical." In the latter years of his active life Monty had indeed delighted in "making his views felt," delivering apocalyptic judgments on subjects as diverse as the Channel Tunnel, the folly of America's campaign in Vietnam and the Homosexual Reform Bill.

¶ From *Monty: The Field Marshal, 1944–1976* by Nigel Hamilton (London: Hamish Hamilton, 1986), p. 939.

". . . Far from helping these unnatural practices along, surely our task is to build a bulwark which will defy evil influences which are seeking to undermine the very foundations of our national character — defy them; do not help them. I have heard some say . . . that such practices are allowed in France and in other NATO countries. We are not French, and we are not other nationals. We are British, thank God!

To condone unnatural offences in male persons over twenty-one, or indeed, in male persons of any age, seems to me utterly wrong. . . .

I am against any suggestion that we should weaken the law as it stands at present. My main reason is that a weakening of the law will strike a blow at all those devoted people who are working to improve the moral fibre of the youth of this country. And heaven knows, it wants improving!"

¶ From a speech in opposition to the Homosexual Reform Bill, May 1965.

ELDRIDGE CLEAVER (1935–)

U.S. Afro-American writer.

The white man has deprived [the black homosexual] of his masculinity, castrated him in the center of his burning skull, and when he submits to this change and takes the white man for his lover as well as Big Daddy, he focuses on "whiteness" all the love in his pent up soul and turns the razor edge of hatred against "blackness" — upon himself, what he is, and all those who look like him, remind him of himself. He may even hate the darkness of night. . . .

Homosexuality is a sickness, just as are baby-rape or wanting to become the head of General Motors.

¶ From "Notes on a Native Son," in *Soul on Ice* (New York: McGraw-Hill, 1968), pp. 103, 110.

STEPHEN T. KATZ (1944–)

U.S. scholar of the Holocaust.

All these facts and factors make plain that the simplistic, inaccurate, claims for parallelism between the fate of homosexuals and that of Jews are to be rejected. Although thousands of Jews lost their lives in medieval Europe simply for being Jews, almost no homosexual was murdered for being a homosexual. . . .

"The Jew" was feared not only as a menacing source of sin — for sources of sin abounded in the orthodox medieval environment — but as a subversive cosmic being whose dark and promiscuous power was demonic. The sodomite was never this; the danger he embodied was never cosmic, the pollution he exemplified never extraterrestrial, the danger never conspiratorial. Homosexuals were immoral, even bestial, and by definition ethically and religiously offensive, but they were never more (or less) than human. Rather, they were all-too-human and hence poor prototypes of the "undoing other." Unlike "the Jew" whose disfiguring charisma lay in his being, the deviant sodomite was merely a sinner — his crime, his criminality, was not similarly ontic. Though homosexuality was closely associated with Manichaeism as a historical phenomenon, there was no great mythic enterprise in which the homosexual *qua* homosexual was implicated, no great dualistic confrontation in which he was cast as the primal opponent of the Good. "The Jew" was the required adversary of Christ, but the sodomite lacked placement, framing, in such a transcendental mythography and, as a result, was not fearsome. One might loathe the homosexual but one need not live in dread of him. "The Jew" had power. This was manifest in his alchemical abilities, his healing secrets, his black arts, his confounded but world-consequential kabbalistic gnosis, and in his verbal-linguistic conjurations.

Witches/women, too were powerful, in particular as sexual beings, mis-shapen healers, and incantators. But gays participated in no like tradition of power, possessed no similar mantic authority, had no comparable, formidable ungodly learning. They lacked all magical (if ungodly) therapeutic skills; they controlled no luminous (if undoing) supernal knowledge. They merely could not control their members. Their offense indicated weakness, not strength, vice, not metahistorical conspiratorial cunning. As a consequence, they were more decried than actively hunted, more stigmatized than physically molested. Above all, the medieval Christian polity never felt itself obligated, because of this constellation of flesh-induced weakness, to organize any sustained campaign against them. Homosexuality, therefore, remained largely an academic concern of dogmaticians rather than an active concern of politicians; a crime against Heaven to which earthly courts, if not law books, paid little practical heed. It was sufficient to call homosexuals names; there was no need to mount pogroms or expulsions as communal prophylaxes against the disorder they represented.

¶ From "Persecution of Homosexuals," in *The Holocaust in Historical Context* (New York: Oxford University Press, 1994), 1:524, 526–27.

JOSEPH EPSTEIN (1937–)

U.S. journalist, essayist, and author.

When you're confused, the whole world seems queer. And so, at various times, it has seemed of late. There have been, as they say, certain revelations. In England it has come out that almost every member of that rarefied and splendid coterie known as Bloomsbury — both men and women — was a homosexual, including, of all people, John Maynard Keynes. . . . More interesting is the observation of a lady intellectual I know who has remarked how noteworthy it is that Allen Ginsberg, Paul Goodman, and many other principal publicists and polemicists for youth culture in America are homosexuals. That is not simply noteworthy; it is fascinating.

In the arts, where homosexuality has never been uncommon — in discrete but significant instances, as everyone knows, homosexuals have been responsible for some of the most magnificent works we have — it has seemed of recent years not merely commonplace but dominant. Camp, a Susan

Sontag production, was in its origin wholly a homosexual phenomenon. Leslie Fiedler, in *Love and Death in the American Novel,* has instructed us that the great American novelists form one long daisy chain of failed queers while the principal preoccupation of our national literature has been a disguised (but obsessive) homosexuality. As recently as five years ago [1965] Philip Roth wrote an attack on Edward Albee, the main argument of which was that homosexual writers ought to stop concealing their true subject — homosexuality — in elaborate and guileful metaphors, and deal with it openly and directly. How quaint that notion seems now! . . . . In the middle and latter part of the Sixties, the novels and plays of James Baldwin, a writer of major talent, began to mix the themes of blackness and homosexuality till it became somewhat unclear which of the two was really the chief source of Baldwin's eloquent rage. Elsewhere and everywhere, films, plays, paintings began to crop up bearing a strong homosexual imprint, more often than not unwrapped in guileful metaphor, or for that matter in subtlety of any kind whatsoever.

In the increasingly large sector of American life inhabited by cultural swingers and intellectual fellow travelers, in which a man is esteemed according to the degree of his alienation from his country, homosexuals have become fashionable, in, with-it. In this world where badges are judged wounds, wounds badges, homosexuals have a deservedly high place, for in fact no higher degree of alienation is possible than to be homosexual in an America whose wider majority culture despises homosexuality without equivocation. There is almost a kind of jealousy of this elite state of alienation, which it might be good to remember most homosexuals did not choose for themselves to begin with. . . .

Still, despite the great ignorance about numbers, current and past, there is good reason to believe that homosexuality is spreading, and will continue to do so. "Rage to your heart's content! Repress! Oppress! You will never suppress it!" Gide wrote that in 1911. But who today is raging? Who's repressing? Oppressing? No one I know, and certainly not most of the writers I read. "Where but in the seminaries," asks Pauline Kael, in the middle of a movie review, "are there still any considerable number of *repressed homosexuals*?" Statistically this is ridiculous, but there is a truth above statistics, and Miss Kael has seized upon it. This truth is, when it comes to repression, why bother? Especially when so many voices are shouting to go the other way — to let it, as a song of the Sixties has it, all hang out. . . .

Not only does the argument between heterosexuals and homosexuals about what is natural and unnatural seem a stalemate, but of late homosexuals seem to have taken to the attack against heterosexuality as a way of life. . . . Heterosexuality has not been without its own special horrors. . . .

Yet if heterosexual life has come to seem impossibly difficult, homosexual life still seems more nearly impossible. For to be a homosexual is to be hostage to a passion that automatically brings terrible pressures to bear on any man who lives with it; and these pressures, which only a few rare homosexuals are able to rise above with any success, can distort a man, can twist him, and always leave him defined by his sexual condition. The same, I think, cannot be said about heterosexuals. With the possible exception of prostitutes and heterosexuals driven by abnormal appetites, the general run of heterosexuals are not defined by their sexuality at all. Although the power of sex is never to be underrated, in the main for most heterosexuals sex beyond adolescence becomes a secondary matter, a pleasure most of the time, a problem only in its absence. Homosexuality, on the other hand, is a full-time matter, a human status — and that is the tyranny of it.

The homosexual's status is that of an outlaw and, even if most of us do not customarily think of it that way, most homosexuals know it is true. Homosexuality has in fact formally had an outlaw status in this country for years, and laws against homosexuality, however unevenly enforced, are currently on the books of all but one of the United States. These laws are barbarous, not to say illogical: when committed by consenting adults, homosexuality is a crime without a victim, and for this reason alone the onus of criminality surely ought to be lifted. Perhaps the audacious and unguent Gay Liberation Movement will bring about the abolishment of these laws — and one can only say, more power to them. . . .

If I had the power to do so, I would wish homosexuality off the face of this earth. I would do so because I think that it brings infinitely more pain than pleasure to those who are forced to live with it; because I think there is no resolution for this pain in our lifetime, only, for the overwhelming majority of homosexuals, more pain and various degrees of exacerbating adjustment; and because, wholly selfishly, I find myself completely incapable of coming to terms with it.

Why can't I come to terms with it? Is it fear of the latent homosexuality in myself, such as is supposed to reside in every man, that makes this impossible? Do I secretly envy homosexuals, not their sexual pleasure, but their evasion of responsibility, for, despite all that I have thought about homosexuality, I am still not clear about whether homosexuals are truly attracted to men or are only running away from women and all that women represent: marriage, family, bringing up children. On those occasional bleak mornings when I should like to drive away from it all, and keep driving, do I hate homosexuals for eluding the weight of my own responsibilities? Do my difficulties go still deeper, are they even more elemental? . . .

They are different from the rest of us. Homosexuals are different, moreover, in a way that cuts deeper than other kinds of human differences — religious, class, racial — in a way that is, somehow, more fundamental. Cursed without clear cause, afflicted without apparent cure, they are an affront to our rationality, living evidence of our despair of ever finding a sensible, an explainable, design to the world. One can tolerate homosexuality, a small enough price to pay for someone else's pain, but accepting it, really accepting it, is another thing altogether. I find I can accept it least of all when I look at my children. There is much my four sons can do in their lives that might cause me anguish, that might outrage me, that might make me ashamed of them and of myself as their father. But nothing they could ever do would make me sadder than if any of them were to become homosexual. For then I should know them condemned to a state of permanent niggerdom among men, their lives, whatever adjustment they might make to their condition, to be lived out as part of the pain of the earth.

¶ From "Homo/Hetero: The Struggle for Sexual Identity," in *Harper's Magazine*, September 1970, pp. 40, 42, 50–51.

ANITA BRYANT (1940–)

Former Miss Oklahoma, anti-gay campaigner, and founder of Save Our Children, Inc.

[From Bryant's 1977 campaign to repeal a Florida law which prohibited discrimination on the basis of sexual orientation]:

[This ordinance] puts the law on the side of the unrighteous. If homosexuals are allowed to change the law in their favor, why not prostitutes, thieves and murderers?

Homosexuality is an abomination to the Lord. . . . Homosexuals will recruit our children.

[Because gays cannot have children], they can only recruit children, and this is what they want to do. Some of the stories I could tell you of child recruitment and child abuse by homosexuals would turn your stomach.

¶ Quoted in "Anita Bryant Is Mad about Gays" by Morton Kondracke, in *New Republic*, May 7, 1977, p. 14.

This is not my battle, it's God's battle.
I don't hate homosexuals. I love homosexuals. It's the sin of homosexuality I hate.

¶ Quoted in "God's Crusader" by Richard Steele, in *Newsweek*, June 6, 1977, pp. 20, 21.

The Lord is on our side. We know that homosexuality is an abomination.
[Gays are] human garbage.

¶ Quoted in "Battle Over Gay Rights" by Tom Mathews, in *Newsweek*, June 6, 1977, pp. 20–22.

[From her victory speech at the Miami Beach Holiday Inn, when the gay-rights provision was repealed]:
Tonight the laws of God and the cultural values of man have been vindicated. The people of Dade Country — the normal majority — have said enough is enough is enough. . . . We will now carry our fight against similar laws throughout the nation that attempt to legitimize a lifestyle that is both perverse and dangerous to the sanctity of the family, dangerous to our children, dangerous to our freedom of religion and freedom of choice, dangerous to our survival as one nation under God.

¶ Quoted in *Conduct Unbecoming: Gays and Lesbians in the U.S. Military* by Randy Shilts (New York: St. Martin's, 1993), p. 300.

JIMMY SWAGGART (1935–)

U.S. television evangelist.

"Homosexuality . . . came out of the bathroom, into the bathhouse, and now into the blood bank, and we have AIDS."

THE REVEREND JERRY FALWELL (1933–)

Former presidential candidate, leader of the U.S. religious/political movement the Moral Majority.

President Carter has given undue recognition to homosexuals, to a perverted life-style, giving them unreasonable privileges. It is something the President does not have to do, popularizing the existence of this "minority."

¶ During the 1980 presidential campaign.

So-called gay folks [would] just as soon kill you as look at you.

¶ From a speech given against the anti-discrimination ordinance of Miami in 1977, quoted in "Battle Over Gay Rights" by Tom Mathews, in *Newsweek*, June 6, 1977, p. 22.

Stop the Gays *dead* in their perverted tracks.

¶ From a direct-mail letter distributed during the 1984 presidential campaign.

In San Francisco we actually saw homosexuals sharing a public platform in Union Square with transvestites, Communists, Central American terrorists, punk rock anarchists, unionized prostitutes, people who would legalize marijuana, and other radicals. Perversion is open, public and pervasive. The main streets are dominated by garish, hardcore theaters promoting homosexual pornography and live, nude homosexual shows. Sadomasochistic "demonstrations" are carried out on stage. Men kiss, tongues entwined, openly in public. Other men wear women's clothing, makeup, and hair styles. Bathhouses, massage parlors, and leathershops are seen everywhere. City parks have become cesspools of perverted behavior. The smell of marijuana alarms the senses as one walks along sidewalks in front of stores like Macy's and Saks. . . .

And you see, what they plan for you and your children is what makes them most dangerous!! . . . and they do have eyes on your children. Remember, since homosexuals cannot have children of their own, the only way for them to expand their ranks is to recruit your children and mine. . . . It is time to take a stand. . . . With your help I will launch a "truth campaign" to counter the homosexual attack on America.

¶ From a direct-mail letter distributed during the 1984 presidential campaign.

AIDS is God's judgment on a society that does not live by His rules. If the Reagan administration does not put its full weight against this, what is now a gay plague in this country, I feel that a year from now, President Ronald Reagan, personally, will be blamed for allowing this awful disease to break out among the innocent American public.

¶ From Falwell's *Liberty Report*, 1980s.

PAT ROBERTSON (1930–)

U.S. journalist and presidential candidate.

"We have a bankruptcy of morality and AIDS is the consequence."

MIDGE DECTER (1927–)

U.S. journalist, editor, and author.

Beyond issues of body and dress, the homosexuals' mockery was outspoken and intentional, and included self-mockery as well. I am referring here to the manner of speech, gesture, and home decoration known as "camp." . . .

. . . The main thing is that it is entirely a homosexual creation, a brilliant expression of homosexual aggression against the heterosexual world. . . .

Like many intended insults, camp came to be naively taken over by many of its victims. Middle-class suburban audiences have for years been applauding homosexual plays for being profound statements about themselves and their lives: consider the kudos heaped on the works of Tennessee Williams, Edward Albee, and others, for presenting what could only have been homosexual relationships as the deeper truth about love in our time. Women have permitted themselves to be rendered breastless, and men to become pocketbook carriers, by homosexual designers. And trend-mongering heterosexuals have embraced camp within their repertoire of taste.

. . . [E]ven the so evidently lesser of the homosexual communities had an air of sportiness, of freedom from financial care, that the heterosexuals did not feel. This air was based in reality, of course. The money, however limited, that the homosexual had in his pocket was, all of it, for him to spend on himself. No households of wives and children requiring security; no entailments of school bills, doctor and dentist bills; no lifetime of acquiring the goods needed for family welfare and the goods desired for family entertainment, with a margin left over for that greatest of all heterosexual entailments, the Future: no such households burdened the overwhelmingly vast majority of homosexuals. Thus their smooth and elegant exteriors, unmussed by traffic with the detritus of modern family existence, constituted a kind of sniggering reproach to their striving and harried straight brothers. See what you have got yourself into, they seemed to be saying, no wonder you have so much less for yourself — and look it.

. . . [W]hatever one's theory of the nature and origins of homosexuality, it is undeniable that the homosexual community boasts . . . an unaccountably high proportion of extremely talented persons. Does homosexuality have the effect of releasing talent, or is it that the talented are more inclined to be homosexual? Like the argument about the physiological versus the psychological genesis of homosexuality, the question bores. The concrete reality, however, does not.

Nor is this talent confined to work. There is such a thing, for example, as a unique and entirely characteristic homosexual form of wit. It is difficult to describe and analyze — as is any form of wit — but unmistakable. Its central characteristic is malice, but that does not describe it either, for the malice is of a special kind, brilliantly playful and startling in equal measure. . . .

The meaning of those undeniable marks of dread that collected around the boundaries of the homosexuals' actual erotic life, then, is that for many if not all of them homosexuality represented a flight from women far more than a wholehearted embrace of men. This was understood in her bones by every heterosexual woman. . . .

The desire to escape from the sexual reminder of birth and death, with its threat of paternity — that is, the displacement of oneself by others — was the main underlying desire that sent those Fire Island homosexuals into the arms of other men. Had it been the opposite desire — that is, the positive attraction to the manly — at least half the boutiques would long since have been out of business, half the alcohol (and latterly, the drugs) would have remained unconsumed, and gay bars might, even under the watchful eyes of the police, have been reasonably sociable places. . . .

Drugs, then, have helped to bring to full fruition the kind of promiscuity that is implicit in the homosexual's flight from women. Without indulging in those high cascades of rhetoric about commitment and mental health that have in our time so damagingly solemnized the discussion of sex, one can say that a chemically-driven obsessive sex life is in its way no less an escape from sexual connection than a chemically inhibited one. The statistics here are more than impressive. In a study of homosexuals in the San Francisco area, conducted by two researchers from the Kinsey Institute [Alan P. Bell and Martin Weinberg in *Homosexualities*, 1978], half the men claimed to have had sex with at least 500 different people. To have had, say, fifty lovers would be a wide range of experience; to have had more than 500 bespeaks the obliteration of all experience, if not, indeed, of oneself.

That many homosexuals are nowadays engaged in efforts at self-obliteration becomes increasingly apparent. There is the appalling rate of suicides among them, suicides attempted and suicides successfully committed. . . . Short of outright self-murder, there is the other quite literal obliteration, through surgery, of the most fundamental ground of one's identity, namely, one's gender. Transsexual operations cannot be very numerous in relation to the size of the homosexual population, but they have become numerous enough — and what is more important, commonplace enough in the public mind — to be a significant sign of something. They, too, have come to represent a possibility, extreme but ever-present, for doing away with an existence that has become hateful.

Most of all, however, there is the extraordinary, growing assimilation into the everyday homosexual world of the twin pathologies of the need to brutalize and the need to be brutalized — the newly ubiquitous S-M. The extent of these pathologies, or if you will, this pathology, is a matter of some controversy. . . .

. . . [T]he question of whether S-M has become a majority, or still remains a minority, taste is somewhat beside the point. Which is, that unquestionably the pathology has grown and spread far beyond its former confinement to the realm of mere kinkiness. . . .

What indeed has happened to the homosexual community I used to know — they who only a few short years ago were characterized by nothing so much as a tender, sweet, vain, pouting, girlish attention to the youth and beauty of their bodies? Whose obsession was adolescent play, and whose safety valve for that obsession was alcohol? Whose primary pleasure was in dress and decor and all things that covered their world with a sparkling if ambiguous surface?

They have "come out," as the saying goes, with a mighty and terrible bang. No longer allowed to hint, to insinuate, to keep private counsel — for hinting, insinuating, keeping private counsel are now politically forbidden marks of repression — they have lost their lightness of touch, and with it, whatever lightness of heart it made possible. Having been defined, or defined themselves, as political victims, they must turn their way of living into an ideology and stand four-square behind it. In other words, thanks to Gay Lib, what was once a strategy of flight, tricky and absorbing, has been transformed into a tactic of frontal assault. . . .

. . . Having to some extent succeeded in staying the hand of the cops — in New York, they now annually play softball together — can it be that they feel the need to supply for themselves the missing ration of brutality? Having to a very great extent overcome the revulsion of common opinion, are they left with some kind of unappeased hunger that only their own feelings of hatefulness can now satisfy?

One thing is certain. To become homosexual is a weighty act. Taking oneself out of the tides of ordinary mortal existence is not something one does from any longing to think oneself ordinary (but only following a different "lifestyle"). Gay Lib has been an effort to set the weight of that act at naught, to define homosexuality as nothing more than a casual option among options. In accepting the movement's terms, heterosexuals have only raised to a nearly intolerable height the costs of the homosexual's flight from normality. Faced with the accelerating round of drugs, S-M, and suicide, can either the movement or its heterosexual sympathizers imagine that they have done anyone a kindness?

¶ From "The Boys on the Beach," in *Commentary*, September 1980, pp. 39–41, 43–44, 46–48.

ALEX COMFORT, M.B., PH.D. (1920–)

American sexologist (THE JOY OF SEX).

If a Martian was writing a history of human idiocy, he'd start with sexual behavior. . . . All human beings are able in some circumstances to relate sexually to members of their own sex as well as to the other. This is probably true of most other mammals (though these use homosexual-looking behaviors for special purposes). It is only odd or anomalous biologically if, like some theologians, you think that reproduction is the only function of sex: in Man and many apes it isn't — bonding, or the expression of dominance, are equally important uses of what we regard as mating.

In all societies and at all times, a certain proportion of people have related more easily, or preferentially, to their own sex and not to the other. This behavior has been differently received. In some cultures it has been simply an accepted variation which anyone might move into and out of: Spartan or Japanese warriors balled their squires on campaigns, and thereby bonded them into the warrior group; classical Athenians reckoned that men should have one kind of sexual relation with boys and another kind with women. In others, the preference made one a wizard. Our own, influenced by Jewish fears of the "unnatural" and Christian hatred of sex generally, has hanged, burned, tortured and persecuted for centuries anyone who was rash enough to express this preference in action, or even in words. We have only just quit doing this. Homosexuals overlapped with witches and heretics, excited the same fears, and got similarly treated.

After hundreds of years of idiotic persecution, it's no wonder that people aware of similar preferences today have started Gay Liberation and demanded the right to do their own thing. Of course they have a right, but the campaign is unfortunate in that it reinforces the totally erroneous idea that there are two kinds of people, straight and gay (older apologists even insisted that gay people represented a third sex). The fact is that all people are both straight and gay if they'd let themselves be; the differences of emphasis have been stamped on by society's heaviest boots so that people are forced into an either/or choice instead of the subtler range of options which are really open to them. Society hasn't bothered too much about the same classification in women, nor persecuted them about it, and in consequence they show much more of the range of normal options and aren't nearly so bothered about relating to both sexes, affectionately and physically.

Some males would call themselves emphatically gay. They prefer relating to, and having sex with, men. This doesn't mean they have a response which others haven't. It means that they don't or can't relate to women. The why of this isn't known — learning, family experience and possibly genetics and prenatal hormone exposure may all play a part, and the convention that if you're one thing you can't be the other hasn't helped. A predominantly gay male who wanted to become heterosexual (some do, if it's a bad trip for them or they feel they are missing an important range of experiences) wouldn't need help to stop being attracted by men, for this is an unused potential present in all straight men which they've trodden on under orders from society. He would need help in overcoming his nonrelation with women. . . .

. . . [T]he [sexual] techniques are the same as in man-woman relations and so are the extras, but a same-sex partner often has a better idea of his or her partner's physiology and uses it very effectively, a thing people with gay experience sometimes miss in straight relationships. If you want your other-sex responses boosted for any reason, behavior therapy can help — but that is learning a new skill, not treating a disease. The whole range of human sex responses is normal and healthy; a less hungup generation will probably use more of it without being anxious.

¶ From "Gay or Straight," in *More Joy: A Lovemaking Companion to The Joy of Sex* (New York: Crown, 1974), pp. 110–11, 116.

ERNEST VAN DEN HAAG (1914–)

American professor, philosopher, and author.

. . . [B]y no stretch of the imagination is the situation of homosexuals analogous to that of blacks. . . .

There is little actual employment discrimination against them, and it is rapidly diminishing. . . .

The attempt to restrict employer freedom in their favor appears to be motivated by a wish for equal recognition, for equal prestige, rather than by a grievance about material disadvantage.

¶ From *Passion and Social Constraint* (New York: Stein & Day, 1963).

. . . There is, of course, a whole range of homosexual styles and personalities, narrower, perhaps, than the heterosexual range. . . . Some homosexuals even manage to have stable and reasonably satisfactory relationships. Many are neither young nor middle class. [Yet I am persuaded] once more that homosexuality, though not demonstrably a disease, is a developmental defect, minor and well-managed in some cases, crippling in others.

¶ From a letter written in response to Midge Decter's "Boys on the Beach," in *Commentary*, December 1980, p. 6.

LADY WOOTTON (1897–1988)

Peeress in the British House of Lords.

[Lady Wootton discussing the Homosexual Reform Bill]:
What are the opponents of this Bill afraid of? They cannot be afraid that these disgusting practices will be thrown upon their attention, because these acts are legalised only if they are performed in private. They cannot be afraid that there will be a corruption of youth, because these acts will be legalised only if they are performed between consenting adults. And obviously, they cannot be afraid, as they might be afraid in the case of illicit heterosexual intercourse, that such action will result in irresponsible procreation. I can only suppose that the opponents of this Bill will be afraid that their imagination will be tormented by visions of what will be going on elsewhere. Surely, if that is so, that is their own private misfortune, and no reason for imposing their personal standards of taste and morality on the minority of their fellow citizens who can find sexual satisfaction only in relations with their own sex.

¶ July 1967, quoted in *The Other Love: An Historical and Contemporary Survey of Homosexuality in Britain* by H. Montgomery Hyde (London: Heinemann, 1970).

JACK WYRTZEN

Head of Word of Life International, an evangelical group.

[From a speech attacking the Miami anti-discrimination ordinance]:
Homosexuality is a sin so rotten, so low, so dirty that even cats and dogs don't practice it.

¶ Quoted in "Battle Over Gay Rights" by Tom Mathews, in *Newsweek*, June 6, 1977, p. 22.

FIRST EARL OF MOUNTBATTEN (1900–1979)

British soldier and war hero.

In 1952 he was denounced as a Communist agent. . . . They also reported that he was homosexual and had been so for many years.

This was no news to Mountbatten; the matter had always seemed to him of little importance. On one occasion he was told that his naval servant was homosexual. "Of course," he replied, "All the best valets are." The fact that Murphy was constantly around his house, however, and that he also enjoyed the company of flamboyant homosexuals like Noel Coward, inevitably fed rumours that he shared their tendencies. The point, to the biographer, is of considerable significance. In spite of the popular belief that the Royal Navy thrived on rum, sodomy and the lash, the second at least of these was viewed askance by the authorities. To be caught red-handed was the end of one's career; even to be the subject of rumour was an impediment to promotion. If, as *Private Eye* has stated, Mountbatten was a practising homosexual, he was risking everything he valued most to indulge a fleeting appetite. In that case his character was wholly different from anything delineated in this biography.

As a boy there is no reason to believe that he viewed homosexual relationships between his contemporaries with anything except slightly priggish dismay. . . .

In fact Mountbatten preferred the companionship of young women to young men — his riding companions were almost invariably female — but their sex was not a matter of great importance to him. Sex itself was not a matter of great importance to him.

He would not have been pleased to have heard this said about him. In 1975 the *Daily Mirror* published articles about a homosexual ring centred on the Life Guards' barracks in London. Mountbatten was told that his name had been mentioned in this connection. "I refused to take this seriously," he recorded in his diary, "and I said I might have been accused of many things in my life but hardly the act of homosexuality."

. . . . Never would he have sacrified his career for lust. To suggest that such a man was actively homosexual seems to be flying not merely in the face of the evidence but also of everything we understand about his character.

¶ From *Mountbatten: The Official Biography* by Philip Ziegler (London: Collins, 1985), pp. 52–53.

THE MARQUESS OF QUEENSBERRY (1929–)

Great-grandson of the man who accused Oscar Wilde of sodomy in the late nineteenth century, leading to the dramatist's trial and jailing.

I believe these laws will be changed, and that when my children are grown up they will be amazed that laws of this sort could have existed in the middle of the twentieth century.

¶ From his maiden speech before the House of Lords regarding the Homosexual Reform Bill, May 24, 1965, quoted in *The Other Side: An Historical and Contemporary Survey of Homosexuality in Britain* by H. Montgomery Hyde (London: Heinemann, 1970).

LADY GAITSKELL

Widow of the labour leader of England.

As a society, we gloss over many perversions between men and women in private. The law, and society, are very tolerant towards these and turn a very blind eye. Those men who are born, conditioned or tempted irrevocably into homosexuality should have extended to them the same degree of tolerance as is extended to any other so-called perversion between men and women. I do not believe, my Lords, that intolerance towards homosexuals is a hallmark of virtue.

¶ From a speech during the House of Lords debate over the Homosexual Reform Bill, July 1967, quoted in *The Other Love: An Historical and Contemporary Survey of Homosexuality in Britain* by H. Montgomery Hyde (London: Heinemann, 1970).

JEHOVAH'S WITNESSES

International Christian evangelical society.

To homosexuality, then, as to so many other problems of life, the old adage applies: "An ounce of prevention is worth a pound of cure." Each father should take an active interest in his son and help him to develop a strong masculine personality. How can he do this? Most importantly, by setting a good example. As the apostle Paul put it: "Stay awake, stand firm in the faith, carry on as men, grow mightily." (1 Cor. 16:13). Basic is exercising self-control. A strong masculine personality is not excitable, is poised, is reasonable instead of emotional and takes a protective attitude toward those of his family. Also each father should inculcate in his son honor and respect for womankind; this he can do by dealing lovingly with his wife.

Likewise each mother should respect her husband's headship and guard against becoming too possessive or overbearing, for by doing so she may estrange her sons from womankind.

Also, both parents can explicitly warn their children against the evils of homosexuality. Such knowledge of homosexuality is a protection. Where fathers and mothers fail to instruct and warn their sons properly, they may fall prey to designing homosexuals. . . .

Helpful in this regard, then, is appreciating the fact that autoeroticism or masturbation is no mere innocent pastime but rather a practice that can lead to homosexual acts. How so? In that self-induced masturbation may make it easier and more tempting for one to engage in mutual masturbation, which is a form of homosexuality. Sincerely striving against this practice will go far to protect a youth.

Likewise helpful in avoiding the snare of homosexuality is to bear in mind what has been said as to how frustrating and unnatural it is. That it is extremely selfish and hardening can be seen by the way homosexuals importune strangers, by their seduction of boys and by the prevalence of homosexual rape in prisons. The evidence indicates that abnormal sexual desire is far more difficult to control than is the normal desire. . . .

Of great importance is for the homosexual to realize that he cannot please God if he continues this detestable practice. So filthy is it in God's eyes that in the Bible such morally unclean persons are called dogs. . . .

Homosexuality is increasing in spite of its being a wrong, unnatural and frustrating way of life. Those in bondage to it can be freed from it if they really want to. Eternal life is at stake! So by all means, do your utmost to avoid the snare of homosexuality.

¶ From *The Watchtower* (New York: Watchtower Publishing House, 1970), pp. 315–16.

But isn't heterosexuality superior? Do not the design and natural functions of the bodily parts involved make this obvious? Isn't male with female the obvious norm, and male with male the obvious perversion? Homosexual "love" involves practices the apostle Paul must have had in mind when he spoke of things "not even [to] be mentioned among you" and "shameful even to relate." (Ephesians 5:3, 12) Nevertheless, at times he did feel it necessary to allude to those shameful practices at Romans 1:24–27. The present also seems to be such a time. Homosexuality has come storming out of the closet. With a chip on its shoulder, it parades about as an acceptable life-style. But is it? Just what does it involve?

The medical magazine Practical Gastroenterology, in its issue of July/ August 1985, detailed for doctors treating homosexuals some of the practices of the gay life-style. It indicates that mutual masturbation is commonly practiced, as are also oral and anal sex. Other unbelievably shocking practices are explicitly detailed in the article.

It shows that homosexuality can descend into sadomasochism, the joy of degrading and being degraded. For true Christians this life-style is totally unacceptable. The insidious propaganda now flooding out on its behalf must be shunned like the plague it is. . . .

Homosexuality is not an alternative life-style acceptable to Jehovah God. Frequently, both gay and liberal preachers twist the scriptures in futile endeavors to make it seem that it is.

¶ From "The Homosexual Life-Style: Just How Gay Is It?" in *Awake!*, March 22, 1986, pp. 14–15.

Homosexuals who sincerely want to serve God find themselves in a quandary. As one said: "If you are committed to the church and just happen to discover you are also gay, what real choices do you have?"

To learn what is required to be pleasing to God, many homosexuals have logically turned to their clergymen. Are these "men of the cloth" giving the right direction? What is their obligation to the homosexual community? What is their basic duty to all people? . . . .

[T]he Bible condemns homosexuality. No amount of verbal hocus-pocus can make scriptures like Leviticus 18:22 and Romans 1:26–27 disappear. . . .

But in general, today's clergy are like permissive parents: afraid to spank their children because 'that would not be loving.' For decades the clergy have thus undermined Bible standards. . . .

Homosexuals who want to serve God must do so on his terms — terms that are clearly set out in the Bible. Today, just as in the first century, there are homosexuals who have been helped to 'deaden their body members as respects fornication, uncleanness, and sexual appetites.' (Colossians 3:5) Granted, this has not been easy for some, but they have learned to deaden their immoral desires just as many heterosexuals have had to deaden their wrong desires for the opposite sex. Both groups have also been helped by regularly associating with the true Christian congregation, which can support them in their goal to 'repudiate ungodliness and worldly desires and to live with righteousness and godly devotion.' — Titus 2:12.

Clergymen who dilute Bible standards and condone sin are doing homosexuals no favors. They may 'tickle ears,' but they are not living up to their obligation to "preach the word." This is their duty to homosexuals — and to all people. — 2 Timothy 4:1–5.

¶ From "Homosexuality — What Is the Clergy's Obligation?" in *Awake!*, September 8, 1989, pp. 12–13.

PATRICK J. BUCHANAN (1938–)

Columnist, advisor to President Ronald Reagan.

[In discussing the AIDS epidemic]:
The poor homosexuals. . . . they have declared war upon nature, and now nature is exacting an awful retribution.

¶ From the *New York Post*, May 24, 1983.

GEORGE BUSH (1924–)

President of the United States, 1989–1993.

I don't think homosexuality is normal behavior and I oppose codification of gay rights. . . .

I wish the issue would just go away, but, of course, I know it can't.

¶ From an interview during the 1980 presidential election, quoted in *Conduct Unbecoming: Gays and Lesbians in the U.S. Military* by Randy Shilts (New York: St. Martin's, 1993), p. 368.

POPE JOHN PAUL II (1920–)

Leader of the Roman Catholic Church.

It follows naturally from John Paul's anti-determinism that he cannot countenance forms of sexual deviance such as homosexuality. He has no sympathy with the view that homosexuality is a compulsion of nature. There is no compulsion of nature. That is what free will is all about. He sympathizes with the homosexual in the same way as he sympathizes with any other man or woman separated from the supposed goal of physical satisfaction by the invisible frontier of the moral law. The frontier may be crossed, but that is sin, and the frontier remains no matter how many times it is violated.

. . . In his view, the body has great importance in itself, and all of its functions, not least those which differentiate the sexes, are parts of God's design. The distinctions between male and female are therefore of great significance and cannot be brushed aside by the crudities of modern unisex theology. "Maleness and femaleness are fundamental categories," he remarked during one of his 1980 Wednesday homilies, "and they are not interchangeable." This insistence reinforces his rejection of homosexuality as a morally acceptable form of conduct. But, more important, it confirms his view that men and women have radically different, though complementary, roles to perform in God's design.

¶ From *Pope John Paul II and the Catholic Restoration* by Paul Johnson (London: Weidenfeld & Nicolson, 1982), p. 114.

[Pastoral letter to America in response to a pastoral letter by U.S. bishops]: As 'men with the message of truth and the power of God' (2 Cor. 6.7), as authentic teachers of God's law and as compassionate pastors, you also rightly stated: 'Homosexual activity . . . , as distinguished from homosexual orientation, is morally wrong.' In the clarity of this truth, you exemplified the real charity of Christ; you did not betray those people who, because of homosexuality, are confronted with difficult moral problems, as would have happened if, in the name of understanding and compassion, or for any other reason, you had held out false hope to any brother or sister. Rather, by your witness to the truth of humanity in God's plan, you effectively manifested fraternal love, upholding the true dignity, the true human dignity, of those who look to Christ's Church for the guidance which comes from the light of God's word.

¶ From *To Live in Christ Jesus*, a 1976 pastoral letter.

MISS MANNERS (1938–)

American etiquette writer (a.k.a. Judith Martin).

Dear Miss Manners:
I have several gay friends. A few of my friends inquire about the sexual preference of every person I mention in the course of normal conversation. I find this very rude. It is none of their business and is usually irrelevant to the conversation. If I answer "It's none of your business," it is taken as "Yes."

Gentle Reader:
Surely the obvious answer here is a cold "Why, I have no idea. I wouldn't dream of asking about anything so extremely private." This is also the correct answer when one is asked why one's friends don't get married, divorced, or pregnant and how much they paid for their houses.

Dear Miss Manners:
My life partner is a man and my best friend. Even if marriage were legally obtainable between persons of the same sex, I seriously doubt that the two of us would seek to obtain such legal recognition. Our relationship does not include sharing sex, and we both prefer it that way. Aside from that, we relate to a great extent as a married couple. Therefore, I tend to assume that when I am invited anywhere and the invitation includes my "spouse," it is within the bounds of etiquette to take my friend and inform the host that I am doing so. I feel that society has no concern with anyone's private life. At the same time, I feel that I have the right to be as public about my sexual affiliations as heterosexual married couples are. People who also happen to be homosexual desire their meaningful, supportive, and loving relationships to be as recognized as those of people who happen to be heterosexual.

Gentle Reader:
Why did you feel obliged to explain to Miss Manners that your relationship does not include sharing sex? Did she ask you? If she invited you to dinner,

do you suppose she would demand to know what you are likely to do when you go home? The fact is that there is altogether too much recognition being demanded nowadays concerning people's private lives. Miss Manners makes no distinction here between unmarried heterosexual and homosexual couples. Indeed, how could she, as she does not inquire into people's personal preferences when she sees them socially, unless it is to ask whether they are allergic to shellfish.

Nor does she approve of guests informing their hosts whom they will bring. It is courteous to invite two people together who are known to be a couple socially, regardless of the composition of the couple, but the hosts may not know of your arrangements. You can *ask*, "Do you mind if I bring Adam? We generally go together." Miss Manners assures you that she would make no distinction in this matter between this and your saying, "Do you mind if I bring Eve?"

Dear Miss Manners:
My daughter would like to invite to her wedding a friend, who happens to be homosexual, and his live-in friend. But his parents, who do not condone his lifestyle, will also attend the wedding, and I am concerned that tension may result and spoil the atmosphere. Am I wrong to suggest that my daughter invite her friend without his partner? Should I give in and hope for the best?

Gentle Reader:
Let us certainly hope that no guests consider your daughter's wedding to be a proper arena for either condoning or condemning anyone's living arrangements. It is not nice for people to speculate on the bridal couple's private behavior, much less the wedding guests'. Surely the gentleman's parents have other occasions for expressing their attitude. Anyone concerned who feels in danger of spoiling the wedding should decline the invitation. In any case, the hosts should assume that guests will behave themselves. If your daughter otherwise sees the gentleman and his partner as a social couple, she should treat them as one on this occasion.

¶ From *Miss Manners' Guide for the Turn-of-the-Millennium* (New York: Scripps Howard, 1989), pp. 106, 194–95, 605.

RONALD REAGAN (1911–)

President of the United States, 1981–1989.

In his attitudes toward homosexuality, Reagan is a product of his generation and his work experience. Homosexuals were regarded with fear and loathing in the pastoral, small-town world of Reagan's boyhood. . . . Reagan's personal views on the subject were conventional and tolerant for his community at the time, and they have changed little over the years. He considers homosexuality a sickness. He is also respectful of the privacy of others and is not the sort of person who bothers about what people do in their own bedrooms. On occasion, he would tell jokes about homosexuals, whom he referred to as people who were "that way." . . . In 1980, when his talented youngest son Ronald Prescott Wilson wanted to become a ballet dancer, the then presidential nominee was worried about him entering into an occupation he thought might be dominated by homosexuals. In 1981, after his election, Reagan told me he had no concern about his son, whom he knew to be "all boy." . . .

Reagan's political record on civil liberties of homosexuals is much better than that of many liberal politicians. He was repelled by the aggressive public crusades against homosexual life styles which became a staple of the right-wing politics of the late 1970s. In 1978, at a time he was preparing to run for President, Reagan openly opposed an initiative that would have removed homosexual teachers from classrooms and established procedures inviting witch-hunts of those suspected of advocating homosexuality. The sponsors of the initiative, which was resoundingly rejected by California voters, blamed Reagan for its defeat. Reagan, well aware that there were those who wanted him to duck the issue, chose to state his convictions. He carefully opposed the advocacy of homosexuality in the classroom but said that existing laws were sufficient to deal with any such problem if it arose. Working from a draft presented him by Nofziger and Ed Meese, Reagan assailed the civil liberties implications of the initiative and summed up its deficiencies: "Innocent lives could be ruined."

¶ From *Reagan* by Lou Cannon (New York: Putnam's, 1982), pp. 132–33.

Society has always regarded marital love as a sacred expression of the bond between a man and a woman. In the Judeo-Christian tradition it is the means by which husband and wife participate with God in the creation of a new human life. . . . In part, the erosion of these values has given way to a celebration of forms of expression most reject. We will resist efforts of some to obtain government endorsement of homosexuality.

¶ From a speech at the 1984 Republican Party convention in Dallas.

PHIL DONAHUE (1935–)

Television talk-show host.

. . . [L]et's look at one particular form of falling in love: homosexuality. Sex researchers continue to insist that homosexuality is a relatively rare phenomenon *if* you define a homosexual as a man or woman who has sex *only* with people of the same sex. Alfred Kinsey put the number at 4 percent of men and 2 percent of women. But the latest evidence indicates that while exclusive homosexuality is still rare, homosexual *interest* is widespread. "Every one of us has a homosexual side," says Dr. John Money, in the sense that "we can be attracted by both sexes." Dr. Money attributes this element of bisexuality in all of us to the fundamental bisexuality of the human fetus. For the first few weeks after conception, the fetus is both male and female, and it continues to carry the legacy of that bisexuality even after it begins to differentiate according to its chromosomal sex. "No matter what we become," says Dr. Money, "male or female, we always carry with us some hint of our early bisexual (both-sexed) nature. Female genital organs contain vestiges of male structures, and the male breast has its nipples, which do not have the same function as those of a female but are there nevertheless."

But why does this seed of bisexuality develop into homosexuality in some people and heterosexuality in others? Or, as mothers and fathers of homosexuals inevitably ask: "Why is my child gay?" The familiar response is to rip a page from Freud and hand it to the distressed parents. "Typically," says Dr. Charles W. Socarides, professor at the Albert Einstein College of Medicine, summarizing the accepted Freudian view, "we find a pathological family constellation in which there is a domineering, crushing mother who will not allow the developing child to achieve autonomy from her, and an absent, weak, or rejecting father." In other words, controlling Mother plus weakling Father makes Junior gay. Simple as that? Hardly. Although one study does show a slight connection between the family situation described by Dr. Socarides and a homosexual son, the reality of human behavior is far more complicated. For example, Dr. Ray B. Evans, a psychologist, cautions against looking only at the parents' effect on the child. What about the child's effect on his parents? "It is just as tenable," says Dr. Evans, "to assume that the father of a prehomosexual son becomes detached or hostile because he does not understand his son, is disappointed in him, or threatened by him, as it is to assume that the son becomes homosexual because of the father's rejection. Similarly, it is as reasonable to assume that a mother becomes intimate and close-binding with her potentially homosexual son because of the kind of person he is as to assume he becomes homosexual because she is too binding and intimate with him." To further confuse matters, a study of homosexual men conducted by doctors in Boston and St. Louis found that most of them were well adjusted, and most reported that their fathers, not their mothers, were their dominant parents.

In trying to understand the formation of our sexuality, both hetero- and homo-, researchers have recently turned their attention to possible biological factors, especially hormones. If falling in love with someone of the opposite sex is in part a chemical process, then perhaps falling in love with someone of the same sex indicates an alteration in that chemical process. For example, the study in Boston and St. Louis showed significantly lower levels of testosterone in a group of homosexuals than in a control group of nonhomosexuals. Although the results of these tests are hotly disputed in the scientific community, they do at least raise the issue of whether homosexuals who want to can be reoriented to a heterosexual lifestyle. Body chemistry is much more susceptible to change than fifteen or twenty years of upbringing. But at the same time, a combination of chemical predisposition *and* upbringing is far more formidable and resistant to change than simple learned behavior.

Dr. Money, like most scientists today, believes that homosexuality is a function of both nature and nurture. In only a small percentage of individuals, who receive an unusually large rush of masculine hormones *in utero*, does there seem to be no propensity whatever toward bisexuality. But the nurture part of the question, Dr. Money says, is more than a matter of controlling mothers and weak fathers. According to Money, there are three leading causes of homosexuality: the effects of hormones before birth and soon after birth; gender learning that occurs between the ages of eighteen months and four years; and lastly, the lack of sexual and erotic rehearsal play among juveniles. But Dr. Money's theories, like most theories of sex-role formation, are largely unproven and widely disputed.

¶ From *The Human Animal* by Phil Donahue (New York: Simon & Schuster, 1985), pp. 140, 141, 144.

ALAN M. DERSHOWITZ (1938–)

U.S. criminal lawyer and author.

I challenged the following statement about AIDS in a [Norman] Podhoretz column: "Curious, that in an age of ubiquitous pornography and blunt speech, it should be hard to say in plain English that AIDS is almost entirely a disease caught by men who bugger or are buggered by dozens or even hundreds of other men every year." I argued that "When Norman Podhoretz writes that, he does not speak for me, he does not speak for the Jewish community. When the Nazis went after gays in Nazi Germany — the rights of gays were inexorably intermeshed with the interests of Jews. Discrimination against gays today is discrimination against Jews tomorrow."

Podhoretz responded in anger: "The sentence that Alan Dershowitz quoted from my column on AIDS, which he ridiculed by his tone, was factually correct, and I defy him or anyone else to challenge the truth of that statement. My position on gay rights has to do with my fear of the rise and spread of tendencies in this society and in this culture which undermine in a very drastic way the possibility of maintaining the family as the key institution in our society, and of raising our children and our grandchildren in a context which makes it possible for them to live and take their place in the natural chain of the generations."

I did not find his response satisfactory. "There is no room for debate about use of the kind of language that Norman Podhoretz used. . . . That is not language one should use against an oppressed minority in this country. That is a buzzword, that is a bad word. . . ."

I argued against the right wing's being able to co-opt the term "family values," insisting that there is nothing in the liberal agenda that is opposed to the family. I pointed out that much of that agenda — aid to dependent children, medicare, family planning, and affordable housing — is designed to protect families from the ravages of poverty, illness, and homelessness. I had chosen a traditional family life, I explained, but "I am here to defend the right of others to choose differently from the way I choose, because today, if you give Norman Podhoretz the right to tell you that you have no choice but to accept his concept of family values, tomorrow it will be the Reverend Falwell and the Reverend Robertson [who] tell you what your choices are. Today, Norman Podhoretz will tell us not to read pornography. Tomorrow, the Reverend Falwell will tell us not to read Norman Podhoretz."

¶ From *Chutzpah* (Boston: Little, Brown, 1991), pp. 202–03.

An Associated Press story, following the arrest of Pee-wee Herman for indecent exposure in an adult movie theater, gave the following advice to parents to tell their inquiring children: "He was doing things that were inappropriate. He went to a place that Pee-wee Herman shouldn't have gone to, and he did something wrong."

Thanks for the expert advice, but that is most certainly not what I would tell my child. If a child is old enough to ask what happened to Pee-wee, that child is old enough to be given an important lesson in Americanism and basic liberties.

I would tell my child that in the United States, adults are allowed to do what they want in private as long as it doesn't hurt someone else. The police are not supposed to peek into anyone's bedroom window to see what they are doing in bed. That is what we call privacy. Nor should the police be sneaking into adult movie theaters in order to spy on people and see what they are doing to themselves in the dark. . . .

It's never too early to begin educating a child in values. And values include far more than the misguided values of the Sarasota, Fla., vice squad. From what I can gather by reading the news accounts, Pee-wee did nothing wrong — even if the police story is true. Any adult has the right to frequent an adult movie theater. If the police believe that the films shown in the theater are obscene, they have the power to prosecute the theater owner and stop the films from being shown. But the adult theatergoer has done nothing wrong by watching an adult movie.

Nor has he done anything wrong by being sexually aroused by the movie. Indeed, that is a major purpose of these kinds of movies. If you don't think that's true, ask yourself why "triple X-rated" videos are so popular for home rentals.

Will the next step be for police to monitor the home uses to which X-rated films are put? Will TV networks now require their stars to sign pledges concerning their movie tastes and their sex lives? . . .

Indeed, Pee-wee's real sin is that he was caught. In a hypocritical society in which many common practices are criminalized, the real vice is being caught. There is no allegation that Pee-wee hurt, or even offended, anyone. Plainclothes cops, who regularly patrol these theaters in search of masturbators, say they caught him engaging in a "victimless crime." . . .

We are moving ever closer to a "Brave New World" kind of society, where there is no zone of privacy in which an individual can satisfy his emotional, intellectual, or sexual needs without some record being kept by big government, big business, or big busybody groups. The Pee-wee Herman case is just the tip of a very dangerous iceberg. Let us not teach our children to become accustomed to Big Brother and Big Sister accusing us of "doing things" that they deem inappropriate. Let us instead use the Pee-wee Herman case to educate our children about the right of privacy, the limitations of government, and the presumption of innocence.

¶ From *Contrary to Popular Opinion* (New York: Scripps Howard, 1992), pp. 306–08.

PRINCESS DIANA (1961–)

Princess of Wales.

The young Princess of Wales unofficially came of age when she was twenty-six years old, married for nearly six years, and the mother of two young sons. That moment was a turning point in her life because she decided to become involved with AIDS, a subject that was all but shunned by "the great and the good" of British society. Overnight, Princess Diana changed from a young mum who liked to shop or listen to pop songs on her Walkman, to a mature young woman who had created a role for herself.

The metamorphosis came the day in April 1987 when Diana opened Britain's first purpose-built ward for AIDS sufferers, at London's Middlesex Hospital. The *Times* correspondent reported that, remarkably, "she did not wear any protective clothing."

At that time the average Briton knew very little about AIDS. Some believed it could be caught and passed on by touch or kissing or even hugging someone who was infected. The revelation that a royal, like Princess Diana, the mother of two young sons, one the heir to the throne, had taken such an enormous risk with a deadly disease shocked many people. The great majority thought she was foolish at best, and stupid at worst, to have taken such a dangerous step. . . .

Buckingham Palace was torn. Some of the Queen's advisers totally opposed the young Princess's becoming involved with AIDS, a taboo subject never discussed in polite company or at British upper-class dinner parties. In 1987, many Britons condemned it as "that gay disease" which only affected "homosexuals and drug addicts," two groups which received very little sympathy from the chattering classes, many of whom believed the victims were reaping the harvest they themselves had sown. The advisors argued strongly that the public would be unsympathetic and warned that becoming associated with AIDS charities could harm her position as the future Queen. They also feared it could weaken public sympathy for the Royal Family.

But Diana was determined. She pleaded with Prince Charles to bring his weight to bear on her side in the argument. Charles preferred not to get involved, fearing his mother sided with her counselors.

"I must do something. Someone must do something," Diana told a close friend. She contacted charities to produce studies showing how innocent babies and young mothers who had nothing whatsoever to do with homosexuality or drug addiction had caught the disease. Armed with this evidence, Diana returned repeatedly to the attack until she won the day. . . .

"She was the first important person in Britain to show you can touch an AIDS victim and not catch it," says Pamela, Lady Harlech, an AIDS fundraiser of some years. "One cannot overestimate the importance of what Princess Diana did that day. Before that no one would go anywhere near them. AIDS sufferers were treated by the general public as though they were the untouchables, that to touch them meant death." . . .

"HIV does not make people dangerous to know, so you can shake their hands and give them a hug," Diana says. "Heaven knows, they need it." . . .

Some of Diana's friends believe one reason she is so committed to AIDS sufferers is that she has always moved in the social circles which AIDS has struck most prominently — fashion, the arts, the dance, and theatre worlds. She has witnessed the distressing effects of HIV on people she has known personally. One of the few people who showed Diana real warmth when she first moved into Buckingham Palace was Prince Charles's gay valet, Stephen Barry, who died of AIDS in 1986.

¶ From *Diana: A Princess and Her Troubled Marriage* by Nicholas Davies (New York: Birch Lane, 1992), pp. 260–65.

NANCY REAGAN (1923–)

First Lady, 1981 to 1989, wife of President Ronald Reagan.

The Reagans immediately adopted a censorious public stance toward homosexuality [in 1967, following then-Governor Reagan's discovery of a "homosexual ring" in his state government, and summarily fired them]. He condemned it as "an abomination in the eyes of the Lord," and she denounced it as a "sickness" and an "abnormality." Yet privately they continued to patronize their astrologer, Carroll Righter, a homosexual, and to socialize with a homosexual male couple who were frequently invited to the Bloomingdales' dinner parties. Nancy maintained close relationships with Truman Capote, Roy Cohn, and Jerry Zipkin, who once lived with Somerset Maugham; she depended on homosexual men like her hairdresser and interior decorator to define her style and execute her taste. The governor enjoyed telling homosexual jokes and would act them out with a lisping voice and exaggerated limp-wrist gestures. He would take mincing little steps, swing his hips, and act swishy. Truman Capote visited Reagan's office a few months after the scandal broke to plead for the men on California's death row. The governor joked about the homosexual ring within his administration. Turning to an aide, he said, "Perhaps we should trawl Truman through the halls to see if there are any of them left."

"Could you vote for a homosexual?"

"No, I don't think I could," said Nancy. "In order to hold office, you have to be a terribly strong man emotionally. No, I don't think I could."

"Do you not consider a homosexual as emotionally stable as a heterosexual?"

"No, I don't think he would be as strong," she said.

¶ From *Nancy Reagan: The Unauthorized Biography* by Kitty Kelley (New York: Simon & Schuster, 1991), pp. 167, 235.

SHERE HITE (1942–)

U.S. sex researcher (THE HITE REPORT).

What is a close male friendship? There is no word in the language which recognizes this possibility — or for that matter the possibility of close friendships between women. The only word available to "describe" men's strong feelings or important relationships with each other is "homosexual." And yet this word is tied to an outdated view of the world which defines people by the gender of their sexual preference or their function in reproductive sex.

If we lived in a non-patriarchal, non-reproductively focused society, it is likely that the terms "heterosexual" and "homosexual" would be rather obscure and infrequently used. Kinsey pointed out in his works on male and female sexuality that the terms "heterosexual" and "homosexual" should be used not as nouns but as adjectives, and that they should be used to describe activities, not people. Other than that, these words have no meaning. And even used as adjectives referring to activities, the words are vague, since . . . many activities can be shared by either sex and are not gender-specific. Additionally, some men do not fit into either "category," as they like to have sex with both men and women. For them, the word "bisexual" has been devised, but the word is rather unpleasant; in fact, wouldn't the word "sexual" be sufficient for all these categories?

"Homosexuality" is an anti-word — that is, it is known basically as the opposite of "heterosexuality." But the word "heterosexual" is hardly ever used to describe a person; a man is simply assumed to be "heterosexual" unless the prefix "homosexual" (i.e., "deviant") is placed before his name. The whole viewpoint which makes a fetish of gender is out of date. It developed out of the definition of "sex" as reproductive activity.

. . . [T]here is a need here for many more subtle descriptive and personal terms in our vocabularies. What is a "homosexual" act? In one way, men are having sex with other men when they share pornography and discuss how they "have" sex with women, or go to topless bars together. They are enjoying sex together and joining in a form of sexually related bonding. Is caring for another man "homosexual"? In some ways . . . it is considered even less manly to embrace or kiss a man than to have sex with him. Why can't men be close and affectionate? In fact, not only can men *not* touch each other and be close physically, even just as friends, but also they are not allowed to share real emotional intimacy, in most cases. A large part of the problem is our language — or lack of it — and the ever-present fear of being labeled "homosexual." What many men seemed to express a longing for . . . was something new — the possibility that men can begin to see each other in a new way, and relate to each other differently, to become more open, more close, and more honest with each other.

¶ From *The Hite Report on Male Sexuality* (New York: Knopf, 1981), pp. 809–10.

NORMAN SCHWARZKOPF (1934–)

U.S. military leader, hero of the Gulf War of the early 1990s.

In [a] sworn deposition . . . , Major General Norman Schwarzkopf characterized homosexuality as being "incompatible with military service" because it impaired good order, discipline, and morale. The general, a West Point graduate, said that twenty-six years in the military led him to conclude that "homosexuals are unsuited for military service."

After the deposition, Asen [Michael Asen, an attorney with the Maine Civil Liberties Union] and the general went to lunch. Asen recalls that they talked more about the case [in which a lesbian, Diane Matthews, had been disenrolled from the ROTC in 1981], off the record. Although Schwarzkopf used the word *queers* in conversation, Asen understood he was using the lingo everyone else used in the Army. Over lunch, Schwarzkopf confided that although he would deny ever saying it if asked in court he really did not care whether or not gays ended up serving in the Army. He had known homosexuals who were fine soldiers. The policy was something that he had inherited, and it was a policy he had to enforce and defend. That was his job, but if the policy were thrown out tomorrow, he said, it would be fine with him.

Later, Schwarzkopf's on-the-record deposition was part of the evidence that prompted federal appeals courts to rule that the military's exclusion of gays was constitutional. When contacted about the conversation, a spokesman said the general denied ever saying it.

¶ From *Conduct Unbecoming: Gays and Lesbians in the U.S. Military* by Randy Shilts (New York: St. Martin's, 1993), pp. 426–27.

HUNTER S. THOMPSON (1939–)

*Journalist and author (*FEAR AND LOATHING IN LAS VEGAS*), writer for* ROLLING STONE *magazine.*

Neither [Dick] Price nor [Michael] Murphy had any place in their vision [to create New Age spiritual transformations at Big Sur] for the parking lot full of pink Cadillac convertibles that were beginning to converge on the baths every weekend. As Price had looked back on this strange collision course where weekend-long homosexual romps were smashing headfirst into their attempts to bring the world an expanded consciousness, he remembered, "We were not trying to pass judgment on anyone, but we couldn't have that going on and do what we were planning to do. So we would try and close down the baths at ten in the evening. You would go down there in the mornings and there would be broken beer bottles, chaos. We had to clear that out, gays or non-gays, if Michael and I were going to do anything about Esalen Institute. We put up a barbed-wire gate at the entrance. And Hunter, who had a lot of aggression and a lot of homophobia, would first try and explain in a very polite way that we had the lease now. We wanted to do something different."

The gathering of gays had gone from a couple of occasional well-mannered visitors to a virtual turf battle. [Jo] Hudson's view was that "Hunter thought they were invading his scene." Thompson would get theatrical about his nightly patrols, putting on his "shit-kicking boots" and wrapping a blackjack around his wrist with a lanyard and letting fly in a loud boom, "Let's go stomp those faggots!" Most often, his thunderous voice could be heard long before he ever descended to the area where the tubs and sunning tables were; anyone hearing him would grab his belongings and flee.

Thompson's first attempts, Hudson recalled, were quite diplomatic. . . . The first tactic was for Hunter to go down to the baths with his little billy club, sit by the edge, and talk civilly to these people. "He wasn't too interested in what they had to say, though," Hudson went on. "He was playing these guys along. He would get just a little bit more obstinate with them. Then he would take his billy club and just start tapping them on the shoulder to emphasize his words." Thompson's words were that he did not appreciate the gays being down there. "It was not like 'I'm going to beat you motherfuckers up.' It was just this funny little intellectual game. . . ."

As time went on, the number of pink Cadillacs kept increasing, and Thompson did his part to enable the Human Potential Movement with even more violent tactics. Now the theatrics were something out of a cross between *Gunga Din* and a John Ford Western; at the top of the walkway leading down to the baths, he would fire his Magnum into the air a couple of times, bellow, "Let's go stomp those fucking faggots," and descend on the baths with three or four madly snarling Doberman pinschers. "The Night of the Dobermans" is how locals recall it: a mad romp around the baths, maybe thirty or forty naked men doing whatever naked men who are willing to drive pink Cadillacs all the way from L.A. or San Francisco to Big Sur are prone to do. Suddenly, above the boom of the surf, above the riot of their own partying, came the sound of pistol shots, the voice of Hunter Thompson, and enough canine snarling to ice their blood.

As Thompson approached the baths, there was a mass exodus of frightened, partly clad partiers. The parking lot became a *son et lumière*, with flashing headlights and the squeal of tires. Thompson thought it a particularly effective night on the job.

¶ From *When the Going Gets Weird: The Twisted Life and Times of Hunter S. Thompson* by Peter O. Whitmer (New York: Hyperion, 1993), pp. 119–21.

JESSE HELMS (1921–)

Republican senator from North Carolina.

This Senator is not a goody-goody two shoes. I've lived a long time, but every Christian ethic cries out for me to do something. I call a spade a spade, a perverted human being a perverted human being.

¶ From an interview in Los Angeles, October 14, 1987, quoted in the *New York Times*, November 1994.

The subject matter is so obscene, so revolting, it's difficult for me to stand here and talk about it. I may throw up.

¶ Describing an AIDS prevention comic book, October 14, 1987, quoted in the *New York Times*, November 1994.

This Mapplethorpe fellow was an acknowledged homosexual. He's dead now, but the homosexual theme goes throughout his work. . . . If someone wants to write ugly nasty things on the men's room wall, the taxpayers do not provide the crayon.

¶ Discussing the federal funding of photographer Robert Mapplethorpe, quoted in the *New York Times*, November 1994.

What originally began as a measured response to a public health emergency has become a weapon, frankly, for the deterioration of America's Judeo-Christian value system. There's not a chance this bill will be stopped because there's a powerful lobby out there in the media and in the homosexual community, and senators are scrambling to put their names on anything that has to do with AIDS.

¶ Speaking against a $600-million congressional bill to combat AIDS on May 15, 1990, quoted in the *New York Times*, November 1994.

Think about it. Homosexuals and lesbians, disgusting people marching in our streets demanding all sorts of things, including the right to marry each other. How do you like them apples?

¶ In a campaign speech in California, October 28, 1990, quoted in the *New York Times*, November 1994.

She's not your garden-variety lesbian. She's a militant-activist-mean lesbian, working her whole career to advance the homosexual agenda. . . . Now you think I'm going to sit still and let her be confirmed by the Senate? . . . If you want to call me a bigot, go ahead.

¶ Discussing President Clinton's nomination of Roberta Achtenberg, a gay-rights activist, for a post in housing, May 7, 1993, quoted in the *New York Times*, November 1994.

NEWT GINGRICH (1944–)

Republican Senator from Georgia, Speaker of the U.S. Senate.

"I don't think their boss ought to ask them about their private life. . . . I don't think you should have a right of filing a Federal lawsuit or having the Federal Government protect you based on your sexual behavior.

"I don't think, as a general principle, that sexual preference is something that you should normally get involved in discussing.

"I don't think this country wants repression [but I am opposed to the] promotion of homosexuality as a reasonable and alternative life style.

[After mentioning the elementary school book about lesbian parents, *Heather Has Two Mommies*, and counseling programs on homosexuality]: "You have had clearly examples of what is, in effect, recruitment in so-called counseling programs. So I am very cautious about the idea that you want to have active homosexuals in junior high school and high school explaining to young people that they have all of these various wonderful options.

"I am not prepared to establish a Federal law that allows you to sue your employer if you end up not having a job because of a disagreement that involves your personal behavior at that level. Does that mean, for example, a transvestite should automatically have the right to work as a transvestite? I don't think so."

¶ From the *New York Times*, March 9, 1995, p. A12.

ROGER EBERT (1942–)

Pulitzer prizewinning film critic of CHICAGO SUN-TIMES *and* TV *reviewer with Gene Siskel.*

The new thriller *Basic Instinct* is under attack from a gay coalition because all of the women in it are possibly lesbian thrill-killers. Enough is enough, the coalition says. Hollywood has been casting homosexuals in bizarre and depraved roles for so long now that maybe it's time to add a little balance to the picture.

If this protest is seen only as an issue involving freedom of speech, there's an obvious response: Hollywood has a right to make the movies it wants, and any group has the right to protest them. That was the tidy conclusion arrived at the other day in a serene editorial in the *New York Times*. I agree.

But, come on. The free-speech issue can be taken for granted. The people protesting this film have a different point. They're not trying to prevent Hollywood from making movies. They're asking that the most powerful image-building machinery in the world stop grinding out killer dykes and twisted homo sex fiends as if sexual orientation had anything to do with criminal behavior.

I don't have the statistics to prove it, but my guess is that gay people, as a group, are less prone to violence than the general run of the population. You wouldn't gather that, however, from most of the movies that are made. Hollywood loves to add a touch of spice to its thrillers by adding a gay touch or two. . . .

The screenplay, by Joe Eszterhas, uses the lesbian angle only for sensationalism. It is not necessary to the movie for any of the women to be homosexual; they could easily be your ordinary straight murderesses. The plot, revolving around the policeman's discovery that he is powerfully attracted to the weird sadomasochistic thrill-seeking of the heroine, is, despite the $3 million price paid for it, not especially original. William Friedkin made a movie in 1980 named *Cruising*, which starred Al Pacino as a cop who was drawn into the male homosexual SM underworld of New York. This is the flip side.

Searching my memory of recent movies in which homosexuals are portrayed in a nonsensational light, I immediately recall *Longtime Companion*, the story of a generation facing AIDS. The women in *Personal Best*, *Lianna*, and *Desert Hearts* were all presented in a thoughtful way. They are the exceptions. Most Hollywood movies present lesbians in a way designed to titillate straight male fantasies. Male homosexuals, on the other hand, are almost never seen in an overtly sexual light; they're usually villains or objects of ridicule.

If a racial or ethnic group were so consistently singled out for sensationalistic exploitation, there would be an immediate outcry — not least from such proud liberals as Michael Douglas, the star of *Basic Instinct*. If they were routinely depicted as deranged homicidal perverts, and if their sexuality was of interest only to the degree that it titillated the voyeurism of the mainstream, we would all be able to see the unfairness. Why are we so slow to get the message about how gays feel?

Movies like *Basic Instinct* are defended on the high ground of free speech, but that's not where the true issue resides. Nobody is trying to prevent such movies from being made. The question is, will Hollywood ever make major productions involving gays and lesbians who are portrayed in a more balanced light?

And what about the major stars who defend their right to be top-grossing box-office winners that use sexual sensationalism as a selling point? Douglas says he sees nothing offensive about *Basic Instinct.* In that case, is he prepared to take one of the gay roles the next time around?

Use a little empathy. It's human nature to take pride in one's self-identity. Hell, every time I see the Chicago skyline in a movie, I'm glad other moviegoers will see what a good-looking city I live in. That's me the Chicagoan. When I see newspaper movies, I'm glad other viewers can see what a romantic and noble profession I follow. That's me the journalist. If I were Latino, I would take pride in *Stand and Deliver.* If I were black, I would cheer *Glory.* If I were British, *Chariots of Fire* would touch me deeply, and if I were a Viet combat veteran I would be glad someone told my story in *Platoon.* But if I were gay, what movies could I see that would not mock and degrade me?

That's all it's really about.

¶ From "On Gay Bashing in Movies," in *Roger Ebert's Movie Companion, 1993 Edition* (Kansas City: Andrews & McMeel, 1993), pp. 801–02.

LYNN JOHNSTON (1947–)

Popular cartoonist (FOR BETTER OR FOR WORSE).

In April 1993, I did a four-week story that really caused quite a stir! . . . Lawrence had been Michael Patterson's close friend and neighbor for many years. He has always been "the kid next door." For the longest time, he appeared consistently with Michael and his friends — but a few years ago, I began to find it harder and harder to bring Lawrence into the picture. Somehow, his life had taken a different turn and I couldn't quite understand why he wasn't still part of the gang. I began to concentrate on him, see his room, his things, his life.

I know all of these people so well. I know where their houses are, what their furniture's like, where they work. I know their voices and their mannerisms, their thoughts are open to me . . . and yet, I couldn't connect with Lawrence.

After "being" with him for some time, I realized that the reason he was having so much trouble communicating with Michael and his friends was because Lawrence, now in his late teens, was different. Lawrence was gay.

It felt right for Lawrence to be gay. He was like so many people I know who have had to deal with this traumatic realization and who have done so with courage and honesty.

For Better or For Worse has always been a sort of real-life chronicle, a look into the workings of a family and a neighborhood — an average neighborhood that could be in any town, anywhere.

Although I have focused on the lighter side, it has been important for me to explore those things in life that are not necessarily laughable, but things that pose a challenge, things that must be dealt with seriously and worked through.

If the Pattersons were an average family in an average neighborhood, they would at some time be aware of the diversity in the people around them and would have to accept and try to understand those differences.

I felt that I was being true to life and to my work if I gave Lawrence the courage to tell Michael he was gay. I wanted to challenge myself, to see if I could broach a sensitive subject and write it into the strip with care and compassion. I included a bit of laughter, too.

Within a few days of receiving the package, forty newspapers declined the series and asked for the alternative strips. Many, however, for one reason or another never read the accompanying letter (or the strips) and were taken by complete surprise when the story appeared on their comic page and their phones began to ring! . . .

As soon as the first panel ran, both the syndicate and the newspapers were swamped with phone calls. Some installed new systems just to handle the volume. Faxes and letters began to arrive, letters to editors, to Universal Press, to me. A spontaneous, emotional outpouring of opinion flooded into the system, and became, I think, one of the most impressive and intense reactions on record to a comic strip story. A young man admitted to his friend that he was gay and a Pandora's box was opened wide. All of us were shaken.

If I had shown one of the characters shooting another in a school yard, there would have been some reaction, I am certain, but it would have been nothing compared to the controversy started by this story. It totally floored us all.

At first, it seemed as though the response was mostly negative. Letters (that appeared to have been written in haste and rage) accused, threatened, cursed, and damned. Many, quoting elaborate passages from the Bible, included threatening and unprintable messages. "Curious thing," I thought to myself, "that these people felt they were worthy to sit in judgment of others." Some letters came as organized protests (many from people who, you could tell, had never read For Better or For Worse). Some came from people who had been violated as children, equated homosexuality with pedophilia and thought I was in support of something that had destroyed their lives. The opposing points of view were varied, definite, and strong.

Within one week, nineteen papers had canceled For Better or For Worse outright. Editors who decided to run the series were attacked for having the gall to do so. Those who chose not to run it were accused of "censorship." Editors and publishers were damned if they did, and damned if they didn't. They called the syndicate. Editors at Universal Press worked overtime, diffusing the anger, answering questions, calming, and reassuring these people who were being harassed, picketed, and were in the eye of a storm generated by ignorance. Those editors who wished to confront me personally were given my phone number. My phone rang constantly from 7 a.m. to 10 p.m. every day. I answered all my calls. I spoke with everyone who needed to know why, what was I trying to do? Did I realize what I had done?

Editors, particularly from smaller communities, were in the most uncomfortable position. In rural areas, where everybody knows everyone else, they were singled out, their children harassed at school. One editor confessed to me that his brother was gay. He was 100 percent supportive but if anyone in his area knew that he was in favour of running the story he would lose his job.

It was mostly from the United States that the sound was heard. Canadian papers carried the pro and con letters on the editorial page. There were two cancellations and a few letters came to me, but by and large, it was a southern and very religious population that responded first and loudest and with a clenched, unyielding fist.

I cannot deny that it was upsetting. When 1,000 people organized to cancel their subscriptions to a Memphis paper, one editor's bitterness came through loud and clear. I had no right to "do this" to people.

I think the letter that hurt most was one of the first I received. It was from a woman who said she had loved my work for years but I was now no longer welcome in her home. She enclosed about a dozen yellowed strips she had kept on her refrigerator. That made me cry.

All of this, we called the "no" mail.

The people who decided to follow the story awhile, before voicing an opinion, began to respond a little later. By the time the second week of the story was under way, the positive side came forward. The phones and faxes continued to ring, but this time, the mail was an overwhelming positive, "Yes!"

The "Yes" mail came from doctors, teachers, mental health professionals, clergy, social workers, friends, and families of those about whom the story was written.

It took awhile for gay and lesbian readers to respond. It was as if they were waiting to see if I told the story as it really was — or was it another attempt by someone from the outside, patronizing and sensationalizing in order to gain publicity?

The letters that came from these men and women were direct, honest, and amazingly personal. I don't know when I have been so moved. It is not possible to imagine how painful it is to be persecuted and reviled because you are different. These letters were evidence of that.

As the mail arrived, my assistant and I sorted the letters into boxes marked "Yes," "No," and "Articles." (We had many, many newspaper clippings!) Altogether, over 2,500 personal letters were counted, and, of these responses, over 70 percent were positive.

All of these letters were answered. All of them were read with respect and interest.

I recently turned these "boxes of emotion" over to the sociology department of our local university, where they are proving to be an intimate and invaluable insight into this side of our human nature.

I learned a great deal when we ran the Lawrence story. I learned that the comics page is a powerful communicator. I learned that people read our work and care about what we say. We all look forward every day to that one page in the paper where the small truths lie, hoping for a laugh, or a little sarcasm, or a punchline that will ease the burden just a bit. I learned that our work is taken seriously, and despite the reduction in numbers and size, the comics matter a great deal. Those of us who produce these panels have a responsibility to ourselves, our syndicates, our publishers, and our audience to use this space with conscience and with care.

I believe I did that with this story.

I believe it made a difference.

My syndicate and many editors allowed me to take a risk . . . and yes, without question, it was the right thing to do!

¶ From "Lawrence's Story," in *It's the Thought That Counts . . . For Better or For Worse Fifteenth Anniversary Collection* (Kansas City: Andrews & McMeel, 1994), pp. 106–08.

For Better or For Worse® **by Lynn Johnston**

For Better or For Worse® **by Lynn Johnston**

For Better or For Worse® **by Lynn Johnston**

For Better or For Worse® by Lynn Johnston

For Better or For Worse® by Lynn Johnston

For Better or For Worse® by Lynn Johnston

For Better or For Worse® by Lynn Johnston

For Better or For Worse® **by Lynn Johnston**

For Better or For Worse® **by Lynn Johnston**

For Better or For Worse® **by Lynn Johnston**

For Better or For Worse® **by Lynn Johnston**

For Better or For Worse® **by Lynn Johnston**

For Better or For Worse® **by Lynn Johnston**

For Better or For Worse® **by Lynn Johnston**

For Better or For Worse® **by Lynn Johnston**

For Better or For Worse® **by Lynn Johnston**

For Better or For Worse® **by Lynn Johnston**

For Better or For Worse® **by Lynn Johnston**

For Better or For Worse® **by Lynn Johnston**

For Better or For Worse® **by Lynn Johnston**

For Better or For Worse® **by Lynn Johnston**

For Better or For Worse® **by Lynn Johnston**

For Better or For Worse® **by Lynn Johnston**

For Better or For Worse® **by Lynn Johnston**

For Better or For Worse® **by Lynn Johnston**

For Better or For Worse® **by Lynn Johnston**

For Better or For Worse® **by Lynn Johnston**

DR. RUTH WESTHEIMER (1928–)

Radio sex therapist and best-selling author.

Many people, gay or straight, are sexually promiscuous. Especially when young. And during this phase they can get into a sex-for-sex-alone pattern that is hard to break. They find it hard to relate seriously to others as love partners.

Straight people have a great curiosity at one time or another about what gays "do." There is less of this curiosity now because so many books have been published about gay behaviour, full of specific gay sex. And this way people have learned that gays do the same things straight sex partners do with the exception of putting a penis into a vagina.

Gays masturbate, they masturbate each other, they have oral sex, they rub against each other and have anal sex. They use dildos and vibrators and other substitutes for the erect penis.

They use fantasy and have a variety of relationships including long-term, short-term, one-night stands, quickies with total strangers (male gays more than lesbians). In these relationships they act like other sexually active people. Sometimes they are good to each other, sometimes not. They have tender feelings, romantic feelings, want security and reassurance, and sometimes they get bored and let a relationship go to pot. Like the rest of us, they do the right things and the wrong things.

The stereotype of a male homosexual that was once popular as a weak, effeminate, "pretty" man, may still exist in some people's minds, but the reality is that gay men are as varied in personality and life-style as straight men. The myth that every homosexual man had an overpowering, domineering mother and a weak, submissive father has long since been debunked, partly by the recognition of the obvious fact that many homosexual men have brothers who grew up in the same home who are totally heterosexual.

Similarly the myth that all lesbians are man-haters who at the same time somehow wish they could *be* men has pretty much faded away as more and more gay women have "come out of the closet" and revealed themselves to be very feminine, well-adjusted women who interact quite well with both men and women.

Few people worry any longer that if a little boy spends a rainy afternoon helping his sister arrange the furniture in her dollhouse he will grow up to be gay, or that if a little girl pitches for the local softball team she is bound to grow up to be a lesbian.

With the new freedom in roles and role models, society has increasingly accepted the fact that men are not any less masculine if they cry at weddings and sad movies, and that women are no less feminine if they are capable of changing a light bulb or fixing a carburetor.

Homosexuality and heterosexuality are both aspects of human sexuality. Sexually speaking, in terms of sexual functioning and sexual relationships, there is surprisingly little difference between homosexuals and heterosexuals. In my work with the Institute for Human Identity I have counselled many homosexual couples and I deal with them in basically the same way that I deal with heterosexual couples. Often the problem and the solutions are similar and sometimes identical.

Perhaps the chief difference is that homosexuals frequently need support in getting their families to accept their life-style and their partners. Since life is more difficult for homosexuals and since many parents are disappointed when they realize that there are not going to be any grandchildren, this aspect of counselling is particularly important. But many heterosexuals also face problems with their parents accepting their partners or a lack of grandchildren, so even this aspect is not unique to homosexuals. . . .

If two consenting adults decide to have a homosexual encounter or relationship, whatever feels good between them should be acceptable.

But it is important to realize that society does make life more difficult for a person who wants to function as a homosexual rather than as a heterosexual. It is much easier, for example, for homosexuals to find social and sexual contacts in large cities that have relatively liberal social attitudes than in small towns where homosexuals may be actively persecuted.

Even in large cities, however, it is not always a good idea to proclaim openly one's homosexuality. Old myths and old prejudices die hard, and though a person's sexual preferences should have nothing to do with the qualifications for a job, or the right to live in a certain neighbourhood, or to do anything else, in real life people do make judgments based on such things.

It is hard to hide homosexuality entirely. Lately many gays have "come out of the closet," stopped maintaining the pretense of not being gay. But the pretense was often no more than a formality. Gays lived as though they had no sex to advertise, but in most cases the people who knew them surmised that they were homosexual.

But not all homosexuals are ready to come out and be counted as soldiers in the gay movement. I don't advise people to declare that they are gay until they are absolutely certain, ready to make a mature choice. Especially not until they are sure what they want to be, gay, heterosexual, or bisexual. I am against pressure in sexual matters, and the pressure to be forced into a gay mold is as bad as any other.

Many people go through a homosexual phase and then into another sexual phase. A homosexual phase may be one of many in a person's life, like a promiscuous phase, an inactive phase, a living-together phase, or a settled married phase.

It also happens that people turn from straight to gay quite late in life.

I don't try to "straighten out" gay people who come to see me for counselling. Many come with real problems but no desire to change from gay to straight at all. But sometimes the problem they bring to me is that they want to change. And sometimes they do change.

There are times when it is wrong to counsel a gay person to try to change, when every indication is that such a change could never really take place and would only cause needless suffering.

My last words on this subject: By no means do I want to leave the impression that as a sex therapist I am lying in wait, hoping for gay men and lesbians to wander into my office, always with the feeling in my heart that it would be better if they could be straight! I only think that people who are confused will be happier if they can be helped to find an identity that will make them happy, or happier than living under pressure to be what they feel they cannot be.

¶ From *Dr. Ruth's Guide to Good Sex* (New York: Warner Books, 1983), pp. 264–65, 266–67, 280–81.